WHERE CHEFS EAT

—

**A GUIDE TO CHEFS'
FAVOURITE RESTAURANTS IN THE
UK & REPUBLIC OF IRELAND**

WHERE CHEFS EAT

—

A GUIDE TO CHEFS' FAVOURITE RESTAURANTS IN THE UK & REPUBLIC OF IRELAND

Chef selection by
Joe Warwick

CONTENTS

KEY

Breakfast
Whether it's a lazy or a snatched one, the chef
couldn't start the day without breakfast here.

Late night
Service is over but the night is still young, this is
where the chef satisfies any late-night hunger pangs.

Regular neighbourhood
Around the corner from the chef's work or home, this
restaurant serves up food good enough to eat regularly.

Local favourite
This is the restaurant that best expresses the
cuisine of the chef's home town.

Bargain
When money is limited but their appetite for
good food isn't, this is where the chef goes
when they're on a budget.

High end
For a special occasion or when money is no object,
this is where the chef goes to splash out.

Wish I'd opened
Professional respect and admiration make this the
restaurant that the chef wishes they'd opened.

Worth the travel
There's no distance the chef
wouldn't travel to eat at this restaurant.

PREFACE

Not so long ago the idea of a restaurant guide based
on chefs' recommendations would have seemed fanciful:
chefs cooked and a cabal of restaurant critics and
inspectors told us where to eat. Although that's still true,
chefs have become empowered beyond their kitchens,
while traditional restaurant criticism struggles to be
heard over the din of an online world where everyone
has a voice.

When it comes to searching for trusted restaurant
recommendations amidst so much noise and chatter,
turning to accomplished chefs makes perfect sense.
Modern chefs are no longer chained to their stoves.
In many ways they're better attuned to their local
restaurant scenes than the average critic, and rarely
travel abroad without where they're going to eat being
top of the agenda.

When crowdsourcing, why not return to the source?
That was the original logic behind *Where Chefs Eat*.
In this exclusive edition, taken from the bestselling
worldwide guide, we've compiled recommendations
for restaurants across the UK and Republic of Ireland
from leading international chefs.

The chefs surveyed were asked to recommend places
to fulfil specific needs: be it breakfast or late-night venues;
cheap or lavish thrills; reliable locals or once-in-a-lifetime
destinations. The result is an eclectic, chef-curated
compilation of guaranteed good meals — an essential
companion for anyone who loves eating.

— Joe Warwick

THE CHEFS

Participating chefs and their restaurant recommendations

TOM ADAMS
Pitt Cue Co.
1 Newburgh Street, London
From a meat-peddling truck on London's Southbank, he has gone on to open his first bricks 'n' mortar barbeque outpost in 2012.
The Black Rat Restaurant **30**..Wish I'd opened
The Clove Club **107**...........................High end
Leila's Café **109**........................Breakfast
Patty & Bun **65**...............................Bargain
Quo Vadis **86**......................Local favourite
St. John Bread & Wine **110**.................Regular
neighbourhood
Tas Firin **109**...............................Late night

TOM AIKENS
Tom's Kitchen
27 Cale Street, London
Koffmann and Robuchon trained, he made his name as head chef at Pied à Terre before opening his own restaurants, including Tom's Kitchen, in London and Istanbul.
Brasserie Chavot **76**............Wish I'd opened
Colbert **56**.................Regular neighbourhood
The Dairy **59**..................................Bargain
Daylesford **55**............................Breakfast
Granger & Co **66**.........................Breakfast
Hélène Darroze **78**.......................High end
The Orange **56**.............................Breakfast
Soho Kitchen & Bar **87**...................Late night
The Wolseley **81**.................Local favourite

OMAR ALLIBHOY
Tapas Revolution
Westfield, Ariel Way, London
With elBulli and Maze on his résumé Madrid-born Allibhoy joined El Pirata de Tapas in 2008, launching the popular Tapas Revolution shortly after.
Bistrot de Luxe **63**.....Regular neighbourhood
Busaba Eathai **83**....................Local favourite
Dinner by Heston Blumenthal **62**......High end
La Fromagerie **64**...........................Breakfast
Khans **55**.............................Wish I'd opened
Locale **60**..Late night

CATHAL ARMSTRONG
Restaurant Eve
110 South Pitt Street, Alexandria
Championing Ireland's culinary culture, the native Dubliner headed across the pond to Washington, D.C., opening Virginia's Restaurant Eve in 2004.
Dining Room **43**....................Worth the travel

JASON ATHERTON
Pollen Street Social
8–10 Pollen Street, London
Created Maze for Gordon Ramsay before going it alone with Pollen Street Social, Little Social, Social Eating House, Berners Tavern and outposts in the Far East.
Baozi Inn **72**...Bargain
Barrafina **82**..............Regular neighbourhood
Goodman **77**................................Late night
The Ledbury **67**.............................High end
Restaurant Sat Bains **32**....................High end
Restaurant Sat Bains **32**.......Worth the travel
The Wolseley **81**........................Breakfast

PASCAL AUSSIGNAC
Club Gascon
57 West Smithfield, London
Born in Toulouse, trained across France, he has founded a London empire based around gutsy foie gras-loving Gascon cooking.
The Breakfast Club **103**....................Breakfast
Busaba Eathai **83**.............................Bargain
Colbert **56**...............................Wish I'd opened
The Gallery **77**................................Late night
J Sheekey **74**.............Regular neighbourhood
The Modern Pantry **96**.............Local favourite

SAT BAINS
Restaurant Sat Bains
Lenton Lane, Nottingham
Chef-proprietor of a cutting-edge culinary destination in the somewhat unlikely setting of Nottingham, England.
Casamia **25**...........................Worth the travel
The Fat Duck **24**....................Wish I'd opened
The Hand & Flowers **25**.....................Regular
neighbourhood
Maroush **64**.....................................Late night

BO BECH
Geist
Kongens Nytorv 8, Copenhagen
Culinary alchemist Bech, ex-Paustian head chef, opened Geist in Copenhagen in 2010, where he serves experimental New Nordic grazing dishes.
L'Atelier de Joël Robuchon **73**..........Wish I'd
opened

HEINZ BECK
La Pergola
Via Alberto Cadlolo 101, Rome
Born in Germany, he worked under Winkler before moving to La Pergola in 1994. Since 2009 he's also overseen the menu at Apsleys.
L'Atelier de Joël Robuchon **73**..........High end
The Botanist **56**..............................Breakfast
Zuma **63**....................Regular neighbourhood

RAINER BECKER
Zuma
5 Raphael Street, London
In 2013, eleven years after opening Asian-inspired Zuma (now with outlets worldwide) and Roka with Arjun Waney, Becker launched Oblix, in London's Shard.
Daquise **69**......................................Late night
The Fat Duck **24**..............................High end
Riding House Café **101**....................Breakfast
Riva **54**..........................Regular neighbourhood
The River Café **61**....................Local favourite
Sonny's Kitchen **54**.....Regular neighbourhood
Wright Brothers **87**....Regular neighbourhood

DANIEL BERLIN
Daniel Berlin Krog
Diligensvägen 21, Tomelilla
Left the Swedish city of Malmö behind to open a restaurant in the heart of the Österlen countryside, where uber-local produce is king.
Hedone **58**...........................Worth the travel

TOMI BJÖRCK

Gaijin
Bulevardi 6, Helsinki
Opened his first Asian-inspired restaurant, Stockholm's Farang, in 2009 followed by three restaurants in Helsinki. His fifth venture, Bronda, opened in 2014.
Dinner by Heston Blumenthal **62**.....Worth the
travel

GALTON BLACKISTON

Morston Hall Restaurant
Morston Hall Hotel, The Street, Holt
Self-taught chef and owner of Norfolk's Morston Hall hotel for over twenty years, he recently opened a fish-and-chip shop in Cromer.
Hakkasan **78**....................................Late night
The Ledbury **67**.....................Worth the travel
The Waterside Inn **24**........................High end

RAYMOND BLANC

Le Manoir aux Quat'Saisons
Church Road, Great Milton
Self-taught Gallic culinary legend and chef-patron at two-Michelin-starred Le Manoir aux Quat'Saisons in Oxfordshire. Founded the Brasserie Blanc chain in 2012.
Shaun Dickens at The Boathouse **33**.......Local
favourite
Texture **66**.................Regular neighbourhood

NEIL BORTHWICK

Merchants Tavern
36 Charlotte Road, London
Former Michel Bras sous chef, Edinburgh-born Borthwick honed his skills at The Square, opening Merchants Tavern in 2013 with Murano's Angela Hartnett.
Cafe Murano **88**..............................Late night
The Kitchin **37**......................Worth the travel
Leila's Café **109**...................................Bargain
Rochelle Canteen **109**........................Regular
neighbourhood
The Square **80**..................................High end
St. John Bread & Wine **110**......Local favourite

ETTORE BOTRINI

Botrini's
Vasileos Georgiou 24, Athens
Holds the reins of his family's long-running restaurant in Corfu and also oversees Botrini's in Athens, and ArtO2 in Thessaloniki.
The Gallery **77**..................................High end

MASSIMO BOTTURA

Osteria Francescana
Via Stella 22, Modena
Culinary traditions are not easily challenged in Italy but Bottura has succeeded with Modena's avant-garde Osteria Francescana.
The Clove Club **107**...........................Bargain

THOMAS BÜHNER

Restaurant La Vie
Krahnstrasse 1, Osnabrück
Strongly influenced by his time under Harald Wohlfahrt at Restaurant Schwarzwaldstube, Bühner opened multi-Michelin-starred Restaurant La Vie in Osnabrück's Old Town in 2006.
Zuma **63**................................Wish I'd opened

ADAM BYATT

Trinity
4 The Polygon, London
Formerly at The Square, Byatt now has two London restaurants of his own: Trinity and Bistro Union.
Bone Daddies Ramen Bar **82**..............Bargain
Brew **55**...Breakfast
The Foyer & Reading Room **76**...............Local
favourite
Meat Liquor **64**.......................Wish I'd opened
The Sportsman **31**.................Worth the travel
Spuntino **87**....................................Late night
The Square **80**..................................High end
Zucca **91**....................Regular neighbourhood

ANDREAS CAMINADA

Schloss Schauenstein
Schlossgasse 1, Fürstenau
The new star of Swiss gastronomy who plies his trade in Schauenstein castle in the heart of the Alps.
Zuma **63**................................Wish I'd opened

DOMINIC CHAPMAN

The Royal Oak
Paley Street, Maidenhead
Head chef at The Royal Oak, he previously ran the kitchen at Heston Blumenthal's Hinds Head.
The Ivy **73**..............................Local favourite
The Red Fort **86**............................Late night
The Seafood Restaurant **25**...............Wish I'd
opened
The Waterside Inn **24**.......................High end
The Wolseley **81**..............................Breakfast

ALBERTO CHICOTE

NODO
Calle de Velázquez 150, Madrid
Madrilenian born and bred, his restaurants Nodo and Pan de Lujo in the Spanish capital fuse Asian and Mediterranean flavours.
Hakkasan **78**........................Worth the travel

SAMANTHA & SAMUEL CLARK

Moro
34–36 Exmouth Market, London
The husband-and-wife team who opened the Moorish-influenced Moro in 1997. Morito, a bijou tapas bar next door, followed.
Dock Kitchen **61**.........Regular neighbourhood
The Ledbury **67**................................High end
The River Café **61**.................Wish I'd opened
Sömine **97**.....................................Late night
St. John Bread & Wine **110**.............Breakfast
The Towpath Café **104**.............Local favourite

ULTAN COOKE

Aniar
53 Dominick Street Lower, Galway
Head chef at Galway's Michelin-starred Aniar Restaurant since 2013, Ireland-born Cooke previously ran the kitchen at Smiths of Smithfield.
Asian Tea House **49**.........................Late night
The Greenhouse Dublin **47**....................Worth
the travel
Kai Café + Restaurant **49**.................Regular
neighbourhood
Kappa-ya **49**....................................Bargain
Owenmore Restaurant **48**.................High end
Upstairs@McCambridge's **50**..........Breakfast
Wild Honey Inn **43**.................Wish I'd opened

OLLIE COUILLAUD

The Lawn Bistro
67 High Street, London
Stints with Bruce Poole and Philip Howard led to Couillaud running the kitchen at La Trompette and Lawn Bistro, joining Peyton & Byrne as the Royal Academy's executive chef in 2014.
Brew **70**..Breakfast
Hoo Hing Supermarket **34**..................Bargain
The Little Bar **70**....................Wish I'd opened
The Square **80**..................................High end
Sticks'n'Sushi **70**.......Regular neighbourhood
Wong Kei **73**...................................Late night

OLLIE DABBOUS
Dabbous
39 Whitfield Street, London
Trained at Le Manoir aux Quat'Saisons, then
became head chef of Texture in London before
opening Dabbous (2012) and Barnyard (2014).
Hereford Road **67**......................Local favourite
The Modern Pantry **96**......................Breakfast
Le Relais de Venise **65**......................Regular
neighbourhood
Tayyabs **112**..Bargain
Umu **80**......................................High end

ANDREAS DAHLBERG
Bastard
Mäster Johansgatan 11, Malmö
The head chef and owner of Bastard in Malmö,
who also goes by the rock 'n' roll moniker of
Andy Bastard.
The River Café **61**.................Worth the travel
St. John Bar and Restaurant **98**............Worth
the travel

PAUL DAY
Sansho
Petrská 1170/25, Prague
London Chinatown-trained butcher-chef-
owner of Sansho in Prague, and owner of
The Real Meat Society (Prague's only whole
animal butchers).
Smokehouse **106**...................Wish I'd opened

GERT DE MANGELEER
Hertog Jan
Torhoutse Steenweg 479, Bruges
Runs Hertog Jan with sommelier Joachim
Boudens whom he met while working at
Molentje in the Netherlands.
Hakkasan **78**..........................Wish I'd opened
Zuma **63**................................Worth the travel

MICHAEL DEANE
Deanes
36–40 Howard Street, Belfast
Belfast chef-restaurateur who, aside from his
flagship Deanes, now runs six other outposts
across the city.
Meat Liquor **64**......................Wish I'd opened
The Raj **42**................Regular neighbourhood
The Sphinx **42**................................Late night

ŞEMSA DENIZSEL
Kantin
Akkavak Sokağı 30, Istanbul
Opened Kantin, a restaurant that focuses on
serving healthy, seasonal Turkish soul food,
in Istanbul in 2000.
St. John Bar and Restaurant **98**............Worth
the travel

KOBE DESRAMAULTS
In De Wulf
Wulvestraat 1, Dranouter
In the Belgian countryside close to the
French border, Desramaults runs In De Wulf
in the area which was his childhood home.
The Sportsman **31**.................Worth the travel

CHRISTIAN DOMSCHITZ
Vestibül
Doktor-Karl-Lueger-Ring 2, Vienna
A veteran of Vienna's restaurant scene, he's
currently behind the stove at Vestibül in the
Burgtheater.
Dinner by Heston Blumenthal **62**....Worth the
travel

MARCUS EAVES
Pied à Terre
34 Charlotte Street, London
Cooks at Pied à Terre in London. Eaves is a
protégé of its previous chef Shane Osborn.
The Gallery **77**.................................Late night
Hereford Road **67**......Regular neighbourhood
Pitt Cue Co. **85**.................................Bargain
Polpo **85**...............................Wish I'd opened
Social Eating House **86**............Local favourite
The Wolseley **81**...............................Breakfast

MIKE EGGERT
Pinbone
3 Jersey Road, Sydney
Originally an experimental pop-up venture
Eggert (ex-Duke and Billy Kwong) ran with
Jemma Whiteman and Berri Eggert, Pinbone
found a permanent Woollahra site in 2013.
The Sportsman **31**.................Worth the travel

FISUN ERCAN
Restaurant Su
5145 Rue Wellington, Montreal
Chef, cookbook author and culinary instructor
Ercan moved to Montreal at sixteen from her
native Turkey, whose traditions influence her
informal, elegant cuisine.
Ottolenghi **105**......................Wish I'd opened

BRAD FARMERIE
Public
210 Elizabeth Street, New York City
Pittsburgher who worked in London with
Peter Gordon. Opened Public in 2003 in New
York, where he now also oversees Madam
Geneva and American grill restaurant Saxon
+ Parole.
Caravan **95**.......................................Breakfast
The Providores and Tapa Room **65**...Breakfast

PAUL FLYNN
The Tannery Restaurant
10 Quay Street, Dungarvan
Opened The Tannery in 1997, following a
distinguished London career that included
running Chez Nico.
L'Atmosphere **50**...............................Bargain
Ballymaloe Restaurant **45**.......Local favourite
Bistrot de Luxe **63**.................Worth the travel
Chapter One **46**...............................High end
Fishy Fishy Café **45**..............Wish I'd opened
Genoa's Takeaway **50**......................Late night
The Greenhouse Dublin **47**...............High end
The House Restaurant **50**...................Regular
neighbourhood
Restaurant Patrick Guilbaud **47**........High end
The Shamrock Restaurant **50**..........Breakfast

PAUL FOSTER
The Dining Room at Mallory
Mallory Court Hotel, Harbury Lane, Royal
Leamington Spa
Trained at Le Manoir aux Quat'Saisons and
Sat Bains, and headed up the kitchen at
Tuddenham Mill before recently taking up the
helm at Mallory Court Hotel's Dining Room.
Bar Boulud **62**............Regular neighbourhood
Bubbledogs **99**...................................Bargain
Duck & Waffle **94**............................Late night
The Fat Duck **24**..............................High end
Kitchen Table **100**.................Wish I'd opened
Pea Porridge **34**......................Local favourite
St. John Bread & Wine **110**.............Breakfast

THRAINN FREYR VIGFÚSSON
Lava Restaurant
Blue Lagoon, 240 Grindavik
Head chef at Reykjavik's Kolabrautin until
late 2013, Vigfússon now heads up Blue
Lagoon's Lava Restaurant alongside Viktor
Örn Andrésson.
Dabbous **100**........................Worth the travel

CHRIS GALVIN
Bistrot de Luxe
66 Baker Street, London
UK-born Michelin-starred chef, Francophile
and co-owner of a string of award-winning
restaurants based on modern French cuisine,
he opened the flagship Bistro de Luxe in 2005.
Bar Italia **81**.......................................Bargain
Le Gavroche **77**........................Local favourite
The Goring Dining Room **56**..............High end
Ronnie Scott's **86**............................Late night
The Square **80**.......................Wish I'd opened
The Wolseley **81**..............................Breakfast

JEFF GALVIN
Galvin at Windows
London Hilton, 22 Park Lane, London
British Michelin-starred chef and co-owner of
seven family-run, French-inspired restaurants,
which he runs with his brother Chris.
Chez Bruce **70**..........................Local favourite
The Foyer & Reading Room **76**........Breakfast
The Gallery **77**................................Late night
Le Gavroche **77**........................Local favourite
Le Manoir aux Quat'Saisons **32**........High end
The River Café **61**.................Worth the travel

ANDRÉ GARRETT
André Garrett at Cliveden
Cliveden House, Taplow
Classically trained in London's finest
kitchens, including spells with Ladenis and
Loubet, he ran the pass at Galvin at Windows
before joining Cliveden House hotel as
executive chef.
Arbutus **81**..Bargain
The Crown at Bray **24**..........................Regular
neighbourhood
Hakkasan **78**.....................................High end
The Hand & Flowers **25**............Local favourite
Meat Liquor **64**................................Late night
The Wolseley **81**..............................Breakfast

MATTHEW GAUDET
West Bridge
1 Kendall Square, Cambridge
Ten years working in New York in the likes
of Eleven Madison, Jean Georges Park and
Aquavit gave Gaudet the grounding to return
home to Boston and open West Bridge
in 2012.
Bubbledogs **99**.......................Wish I'd opened
The Ledbury **67**.....................Worth the travel

ALEXIS GAUTHIER
Gauthier Soho
21 Romilly Street, London
French-born chef-patron at London's
Michelin-starred Gauthier Soho, where the
menu's emphasis on vegetables is distinctly
un-French.
Cây Tre **83**...Bargain
Dean Street Townhouse **83**..............Breakfast
The Ivy **73**.................................Local favourite
New Mayflower **72**...........................Late night
The River Café **61**.................Wish I'd opened
Tendido Cuatro **67**......Regular neighbourhood

ROBIN GILL
The Dairy
15 The Pavement, London
Having worked at Le Manoir aux Quat'Saisons,
Dublin-born Gill's impressive résumé was
further boosted by a stint at Noma. He
opened The Dairy bistro in Clapham in 2013.
Barrafina **82**..............Regular neighbourhood
Beigel Bake **107**..............................Late night
Hawksmoor **94**...............................Breakfast
Honest Burgers **93**............................Bargain
Mien Tay **55**.......................................Bargain
Upstairs at the Ten Bells **111**..................Local
favourite

PETER GORDON
The Providores and Tapa Room
109 Marylebone High Street, London
Fusion pioneer Gordon runs restaurants
in Istanbul, London, and his native New
Zealand, where he reopened the iconic
Sugar Club in 2013.

BEN GREENO
Momofuku Seiōbo
80 Pyrmont Street, Sydney
Runs the kitchen for David Chang in Sydney.
Born in England, he's worked with Sat Bains
and René Redzepi.
The Clove Club **107**...............Worth the travel

GABRIELLE HAMILTON
Prune
54 East 1st Street, New York City
Chef-owner of Prune in Manhattan, which
gained cult status for its gutsy approach
as outlined in her memoir *Blood, Bones
and Butter*.
The River Café **61**...................Worth the travel
Rochelle Canteen **109**...........Worth the travel

ANNA HANSEN
The Modern Pantry
47–48 St John's Square, London
Opened The Providores and Tapa Room
with Peter Gordon in London's Marylebone
in 2001. She launched her own restaurant,
The Modern Pantry, in Clerkenwell in 2008.
The Clove Club **107**.....Regular neighbourhood
Dishoom Shoreditch **108**.................Late night
Dishoom Shoreditch **108**...................Bargain
The Hand & Flowers **25**.........Worth the travel
Ottolenghi **105**.........................Local favourite
Sunday **106**......................................Breakfast

BRIAN MARK HANSEN
Søllerød Kro
Søllerødvej 35, Holte
After manning the stove at Christiansholm
Slot, Hansen returned in 2013 to run the
kitchen at Søllerød Kro, a 330-year-old inn
where he was formerly sous chef.
Dinner by Heston Blumenthal **62**.....Worth the
travel

STEFFEN HANSEN
Grefsenkollen
Grefsenkollveien 100, Oslo
In 2008 he took over the kitchen at Grefsen-
kollen, a timber ski lodge originally opened
in 1927.
VQ 24 Hours **58**...............................Late night
The Wolseley **81**..............................Breakfast

HENRY HARRIS

Elder of the two Harris brothers, he owned Racine in London's Knightsbridge which closed after twelve years of business in 2014.

Le Gavroche **77**........................Local favourite
North China **54**.........Regular neighbourhood
Ranoush Juice **65**............................Late night
The Sportsman **31**.................Worth the travel
Tayyabs **112**..Bargain
Violet **102**.......................................Breakfast
Zuma **63**..High end

MATTHEW HARRIS

Bibendum
81 Fulham Road, London
Has carved out a career at Terence Conran's Bibendum, in Michelin's former London HQ, where he began cooking in 1987.

The Begging Bowl **106**..........Worth the travel
Bravi Ragazzi **112**...........................Late night
The Ivy **73**.............................Wish I'd opened
Joy King Lau **72**..................................Bargain
The Wolseley **81**.......................Local favourite
Yauatcha **88**...............Regular neighbourhood
Zuma **63**...High end

SAM HARRIS

Zucca
184 Bermondsey Street, London
The River Café-trained force behind Zucca, a Modern Italian opened in southeast London's Bermondsey Street in 2010.

Albion Cafe **107**................................Breakfast
Cafe East **90**..Bargain
Magdalen **92**...............Regular neighbourhood
The Square **80**...................................High end
St. John Bar and Restaurant **98**......Late night
St. John Bar and Restaurant **98**.............Local favourite
St. John Bar and Restaurant **98**........Wish I'd opened

STEPHEN HARRIS

The Sportsman
Faversham Road, Seasalter
In 1999 he took over a rundown pub in Seasalter, on a remote part of the Kentish coast, and built it up into one of the England's most exciting destination restaurants.

David Brown Delicatessen **31**..............Regular neighbourhood
Elliott's Coffee Shop **31**....................Breakfast
The Goods Shed Restaurant **30**..............Local favourite
Hedone **58**...High end

TOM HARRIS

Harris worked with the nose-to-tail St. John group for ten years where he won a Michelin star, then went on to retain the star at One Leicester Street, where he was chef-patron until 2013.

Baozi Inn **72**.......................................Bargain
Beigel Bake **107**.......................Local favourite
The Clove Club **107**................Wish I'd opened
Lardo **101**.................Regular neighbourhood
Leila's Café **109**...............................Breakfast
St. John Bar and Restaurant **98**.........High end
Umut 2000 **98**...................................Late night

ANGELA HARTNETT

Murano
20 Queen Street, London
Began her career with Gordon Ramsay before going solo with Murano in 2010. She now oversees several other casual and less casual establishments in London and Hampshire.

Barrafina **82**.......................................Bargain
Brawn **103**.................Regular neighbourhood
The Delaunay **73**.............................Late night
HIX **84**...Late night
The Modern Pantry **96**....................Breakfast
Moro **96**.....................Regular neighbourhood
The Sportsman **31**.................Wish I'd opened
The Square **80**...................................High end
St. John Bread & Wine **110**......Local favourite
Tramshed **110**.............Regular neighbourhood
The Waterside Inn **24**.......................High end
Zucca **91**....................Regular neighbourhood

NIGEL HAWORTH

Northcote
Northcote Road, Blackburn
Has run Northcote with Craig Bancroft since 1984. They also operate five food-led pubs across the North of England, including The Three Fishes at Milton, and The Highwayman Inn at Burrow.

Bentley's Oyster Bar & Grill **75**...........Regular neighbourhood
Clayton Street Chippy **32**....................Bargain
The Fat Duck **24**....................Wish I'd opened
The Inn at Whitewell **32**..........Local favourite
The Wolseley **81**...............................Breakfast

FERGUS HENDERSON

St. John Bar and Restaurant
26 St John Street, London
Champion of using the bits of beast that British chefs tended to leave behind before St. John arrived in 1994. Opened St. John Bread & Wine in 2003.

Ciao Bella **91**..............Regular neighbourhood
Le Gavroche **77**................................High end
London Jade Garden **72**....................Bargain
The Sirloin **98**.................................Breakfast
Sweetings **95**...........................Local favourite

MARGOT HENDERSON

Rochelle Canteen
Arnold Circus, London
Wife of Fergus 'nose-to-tail' Henderson, she is a culinary force in her own right running the Rochelle Canteen in London's East End and Arnold & Henderson with her business partner Melanie Arnold.

Bar Italia **81**...................................Breakfast
Barrafina **82**........................Wish I'd opened
Brawn **103**...Bargain
Ducksoup **84**..............Regular neighbourhood
Hix Oyster & Fish House **28**.................Worth the travel
Ikeda **79**..High end
Royal China **55**................................Late night
St. John Bar and Restaurant **98**.......Breakfast
St. John Bar and Restaurant **98**.............Local favourite

SERGIO HERMAN
Pure C
Boulevard de Wielingen 49, Cadzand
Since closing the legendary Oud Sluis in 2013, Sergio hasn't rested on his laurels, focusing on Pure C, the Cadzand-Bad restaurant he opened in 2010, and The Jane, his new venture in Antwerp.
The Gallery **77**......................Wish I'd opened

SHAUN HILL
The Walnut Tree
Llanddewi Skirrid, Abergavenny
British restaurant legend that put Gidleigh Park in Devon and the Merchant House in Ludlow on the map. Now runs The Walnut Tree Inn in Abergavenny, South Wales.
The Fountain **76**..............................Breakfast
Gidleigh Park **27**..............................High end
The Hardwick **39**........Regular neighbourhood
Polpo **85**................................Wish I'd opened
Spuntino **87**..Bargain

ESBEN HOLMBOE BANG
Maaemo
Schweigaards Gate 15, Oslo
Danish chef of, and partner in, Maaemo in Oslo, who took inspiration from Copenhagen, notably Noma, before opening his successful take on Modern Nordic in 2011.
The Ledbury **67**.....................Worth the travel

PHILIP HOWARD
The Square
6–10 Bruton Street, London
Chef and co-owner of The Square in London since it opened in 1991, he's more recently teamed up with restaurateur Rebecca Mascarenhas at Kitchen W8 (2009) and Sonny's Kitchen (2012).
Hakkasan **78**..................................Late night
Hakkasan **78**....................................High end
The River Café **61**.................Wish I'd opened
Scott's **80**...............................Local favourite
The Wolseley **81**.............................Breakfast
Zucca **91**....................Regular neighbourhood

METTE HVARRE GASSNER
Ti Trin Ned
Norgesgade 3, Fredericia
Proclaiming 'we don't call our kitchen Nordic', Mette and husband Rainer reach beyond borders for inspiration at Ti Trin Ned, appealing to diners' senses with local ingredients and innovative techniques.
Bubbledogs **99**.......................Wish I'd opened

ALFONSO & ERNESTO IACCARINO
Don Alfonso
Corso Sant'Agata 11–13, Sant'Agata sui Due Golfi
Champions of tradition and innovation, they run their family restaurant and hotel on an organic farm, and restaurants in Macau and Marrakech.
Zuma **63**................................Wish I'd opened

ANDRÉ JAEGER
Die Fischerzunft
Rheinquai 8, Schaffhausen
Chef-owner of Die Fischerzunft, Jaeger has brought his unique East meets West cooking to the banks of the Rhine for over three decades.
Coya **76**..................................Worth the travel

TIMOTHY JOHNSON
Apicius
23 Stone Street, Cranbrook
A protégé of Nico Ladenis, Johnson opened Apicius in Kent in 2004, winning acclaim for his imaginative, French-influenced cooking.
Dinner by Heston Blumenthal **62**....Worth the travel
The Landgate Bistro **29**......................Regular neighbourhood
The Pleasant Café **31**......................Breakfast

HYWEL JONES
The Park Restaurant
Lucknam Park Hotel, Colerne, Chippenham
After training with Nico Ladenis and Marco Pierre White, he's been at Lucknam Park near Bath since 2004.
The Eastern Eye **33**.........................Late night
The Fig Tree **40**..........Regular neighbourhood
The Harbourmaster **39**..........Wish I'd opened
The Hardwick **39**.....................Local favourite
Jika Jika **33**..................................Breakfast
The Square **80**..................................High end

JONATHAN JONES
The Anchor & Hope
36 The Cut, London
Co-owner of London's The Anchor & Hope and Great Queen Street, Jones is a graduate of Fergus Henderson's St. John.
The Abbeville Kitchen **59**..................Breakfast
Franco Manca **92**...................Wish I'd opened
Lahore Karahi **69**................................Bargain
Otto's **96**.......................................High end
Roti Joupa **59**................................Late night
St. John Bar and Restaurant **98**..............Local favourite

MIKAEL JONSSON
Hedone
301–303 Chiswick High Road, London
Self-taught chef and owner of Hedone who won a Michelin star in 2012, one year after opening the restaurant.
Franco Manca **92**................................Bargain
The Ledbury **67**.......................Local favourite
Medlar **57**..................Regular neighbourhood
Monmouth Coffee Company **74**........Breakfast

MARK JORDAN
Ocean Restaurant
The Atlantic Hotel, Le Mont de la Pulente, St Brelade
Welsh-born chef who got his first kitchen job with the late Keith Floyd and now heads up the kitchen at the two-Michelin-starred Ocean Restaurant in Jersey.
Big Vern's **36**..................................Breakfast
Siam Garden **36**..........Regular neighbourhood

JACOB KENEDY

Bocca di Lupo
12 Archer Street, London
After a decade at Moro he opened Bocca di
Lupo in 2008, followed by Gelupo, his gelateria
and coffee bar that sits opposite.

A.Wong **70**..Breakfast
Antepliler **104**................................Bargain
Bo Làng **69**.....................................Breakfast
Koffmann's **63**........................Wish I'd opened
Moro **96**.....................Regular neighbourhood
Roux at the Landau **66**......................High end
Royal China **55**...............................Breakfast
Sweetings **95**...........................Local favourite
The Walnut Tree **40**...............Worth the travel

TOM KERRIDGE

The Hand & Flowers
126 West Street, Marlow
Owner of The Hand & Flowers, the former
rundown pub in Marlow, southeast England,
which he took over in 2005 and turned into
a destination.

The Fat Duck **24**...............................High end
The Hinds Head **24**.............................Regular
neighbourhood
Meat Liquor **64**................................Late night
Pollen Street Social **80**..........Wish I'd opened
Terroirs **112**......................................Bargain

MILES KIRBY

Caravan
11–13 Exmouth Market, London
Ran the kitchen at The Providores and Tapa
Room before launching Caravan with fellow
Kiwi Chris Ammermann in 2010. A second
branch in King's Cross followed in 2012.

Afghan Kitchen **104**...........................Bargain
Bone Daddies Ramen Bar **82**..........Late night
The Company Shed **29**..........Worth the travel
Ducksoup **84**..............Regular neighbourhood
Moro **96**.....................Regular neighbourhood
Palm2 **102**..............................Local favourite
Palmera Oasis **105**..........................Late night
Rochelle Canteen **109** Regular neighbourhood
Roka **101**..High end
St. John Bar and Restaurant **98**.............Local
favourite
The Towpath Café **104**....................Breakfast
Trullo **106**..................Regular neighbourhood
The Windsor Castle **103**.....................Regular
neighbourhood

SCOT KIRTON

La Colombe
Spaanschemat River Road, Cape Town
South African who took over at La Colombe
in 2010. Previously cooked at Constantia
Uitsig's River Café.

The Ledbury **67**.....................Worth the travel

TOM KITCHIN

The Kitchin
78 Commercial Quay, Edinburgh
Trained with Koffmann, Ducasse and Savoy,
owner of The Kitchin (2006) and The Scran &
Scallie (2013) in his hometown of Edinburgh.

Anstruther Fish Bar **38**.......................Bargain
Koffmann's **63**............Regular neighbourhood
Ondine Restaurant **38**..............Local favourite
The Peat Inn **38**................................High end
La Petite Maison **79**..............Wish I'd opened
Urban Angel **38**................................Breakfast

JAMES KNAPPETT

Kitchen Table
70 Charlotte Street, London
With a glittering résumé including stints at
The Ledbury, Noma and Per Se, Knappett settled in London as chef-patron of Bubbledogs,
a gourmet hot dog-Champagne concept with
a fine-dining annex, Kitchen Table.

Andrew Edmunds **81**..........................Bargain
Parlour Kensal **62**......Regular neighbourhood
St. John Bread & Wine **110**.....Local favourite
Sushi Tetsu **97**.......................Wish I'd opened

ATUL KOCHHAR

Benares
Berkeley Square, London
Indian-born, British-based chef and owner of
Benares (2007), Kochhar is widely accepted
as the pioneer of modern Indian cuisine.

Busaba Eathai **83**..................Wish I'd opened
Duck & Waffle **94**.............................High end
HIX at the Albemarle **78**.................Late night
Lahore Kebab House **112**...................Bargain
Shoryu Ramen **88**..................Local favourite
The Wolseley **81**..............................Breakfast

PIERRE KOFFMANN

Koffmann's
The Berkeley, Wilton Place, London
Gascon-born, he became a legend in London
at La Tante Claire, opened in 1977. Made his
comeback in 2010 with Koffmann's at The
Berkeley.

A.Wong **70**..Bargain
Le Colombier **57**.........Regular neighbourhood
The Five Fields **57**.............................High end
Le Gavroche **77**........................Local favourite
Raoul's **63**.......................................Breakfast
Royal China **55**..................................Bargain

JEREMY LEE

Quo Vadis
26–29 Dean Street, London
Scottish-born chef who left the Blueprint
Café in 2011 to take the reins at Quo Vadis,
bringing his award-winning combination of
French technique and British seasonality.

The Anchor & Hope **110**.....................Bargain
Bibendum **68**...................................High end
Maison Bertaux **85**..........................Breakfast
The River Café **61**....................Local favourite
St. John Bar and Restaurant **98**..............Wish
I'd opened

ROSS LEWIS

Chapter One
18–19 Parnell Square, Dublin
Son of a farmer, Irish-born Lewis found cooking while at university. He opened Chapter
One in 1992.

Ballymaloe Restaurant **45**................Breakfast
L'Ecrivain **47**....................................High end
Farmgate Café **44**...................Local favourite
Fishy Fishy Café **45**...............Wish I'd opened
M & L Chinese Restaurant **46**.........Late night
That's Amore **48**........Regular neighbourhood

OLIVIER LIMOUSIN
L'Atelier de Joël Robuchon
92 Narathiwas Ratchanakharin Road, Bangkok
Following stints at L'Amphyclès, under
mentor Philippe Groult, and various Michelin-
starred Paris establishments, he joined
L'Atelier de Joël Robuchon in 2006.

Alain Ducasse **75**...............................High end
Aubaine **75**.......................................Breakfast
Augustine Kitchen **54**..........................Regular
neighbourhood
Cafe Boheme **83**...............................Late night
Casse-Croûte **90**......................Local favourite
La Petite Maison **79**...............Wish I'd opened

GIORGIO LOCATELLI
Locanda Locatelli
8 Seymour Street, London
Born into a family of chefs, Locatelli came
to London at nineteen, working at the Savoy
and winning Zafferano its first Michelin star
before opening Locanda Locatelli in 2002.

Beijing Dumpling **72**.........................Late night
Caravan **106**.........................Wish I'd opened
Le Laurent **463**.................................High end
Oblix **92**............................Local favourite
Taste of Siam **93**.................................Bargain
Tinello **56**...................Regular neighbourhood

JAMES LOWE
Lyle's
56 Shoreditch High Street, London
Ran proceedings at Fergus Henderson's St.
John Bread & Wine, worked at The Fat Duck
and Noma, before forming chef-trio The
Young Turks. Opened Lyle's in London in 2014.

40 Maltby Street **90**....Regular neighbourhood
The Clove Club **107**..................Local favourite
Koya Bar **85**.....................................Breakfast
Pitt Cue Co. **85**....................................Bargain
The River Café **61**.............................High end
St. John Bread & Wine **110**....Wish I'd opened

TONY MANTUANO
Spiaggia
980 North Michigan Avenue, Chicago
Chef-partner of Michelin-starred standard
bearer for Italian food, Spiaggia, since
1984, and Lorenzo (Miami), Bar Toma and
Terzo Piano (Chicago) and Mangia Trattoria
in Kenosha.

Dinner by Heston Blumenthal **62**..........Worth
the travel

GREG MARCHAND
Frenchie
5–6 Rue du Nil, Paris
The Nantes native travelled the globe, from
New York to Hong Kong, before returning to
his homeland to open Frenchie – the nickname Jamie Oliver gave him at Fifteen.

Sông Quê Café **104**.............................Bargain

FRANCESCO MAZZEI
L'Anima
1 Snowden Street, London
Opened L'Anima in London in 2008. Born in
Calabria, he first arrived in the UK in 1996,
working for restaurateurs Corbin and King
and Alan Yau.

Bar Boulud **62**................................Late night
Busaba Eathai **83**................................Bargain
CUT at 45 Park Lane **76**....................High end
The Duke of Cambridge **105**.....Local favourite
Hakkasan **78**..............Regular neighbourhood
The Wolseley **81**.............................Breakfast
Zuma **63**.................................Wish I'd opened

BRAD MCDONALD
The Lockhart
22–24 Seymour Place, London
Formerly of Brooklyn's Colonie, Gran Eléctrica
and Governor, acclaimed Mississippi-born
McDonald brought Deep South-influenced
cuisine to London in 2014 at The Lockhart.

The Clove Club **107**.....Regular neighbourhood
St. John Bread & Wine **110**.............Breakfast

ISAAC MCHALE
The Clove Club
380 Old Street, London
Co-founder of The Young Turks chef collective,
Orkney-born McHale worked at The Ledbury,
Noma and Momofuku before opening The
Clove Club in East London in 2013.

Franco Manca **92**................................Bargain
Hoi Polloi **108**................................Breakfast
Kêu Bánh Mì Deli **108**.........................Regular
neighbourhood
The Ledbury **67**.................................High end
The Quality Chop House **96**......Local favourite
Tava Restaurant **97**.........................Late night

NIALL MCKENNA
James Street South Restaurant
21 James Street South, Belfast
The chef-owner of Belfast's James Street
South, opened in 2003, and the Bar + Grill,
launched in 2001, both located in a converted
linen mill in the city centre.

Bistro at Balloo House **43**.........Local favourite
Canteen at the MAC **40**....................Breakfast
Chapter One **46**....................Worth the travel
The Great Room Restaurant **41**.........High end
Mourne Seafood Bar **42**.....................Bargain
The River Café **61**.................Wish I'd opened
Shu **42**...................Regular neighbourhood

JP MCMAHON
Aniar
53 Lower Dominick Street, Galway
Heralded as 'the perfect ambassador of mod-
ern Irish cuisine', restaurateur and Culinary
Director of the EatGalway Restaurant Group
McMahon opened Cava tapas restaurant in
2008 and Aniar in 2011.

Ard Bia at Nimmos **48**......................Breakfast
Galway Farmers Market **49**.................Bargain
The Greenhouse Dublin **47**................High end
Kai Café + Restaurant **49**.................Regular
neighbourhood
Sheridans Cheesemongers **49**.........Late night
St. John Bar and Restaurant **98**.........Wish I'd
opened

NUNO MENDES

Chiltern Firehouse
1 Chiltern Street, London

Portuguese-born Mendes worked at elBulli, Jean Georges and the Coyote Café before opening Viajante and Corner Room in London, then taking up residence at André Balazs's new hotel, the Chiltern Firehouse.

Beagle **103**......................................Breakfast
Bubbledogs **99**......................Wish I'd opened
Mangal Ocakbasi **97**.........................Late night
Raw Duck **102**...........Regular neighbourhood
St. John Bread & Wine **110**......Local favourite
Sushi Tetsu **97**...................................High end

MICHAEL MEREDITH

Merediths
365 Dominion Road, Auckland

Born in Samoa, moved to New Zealand at thirteen and made his name at Auckland's The Grove before opening Merediths in 2007.

Restaurant Sat Bains **32**.......Wish I'd opened

THOMASINA MIERS

Wahaca Covent Garden
66 Chandos Place, London

On the back of her 2005 success in BBC's Masterchef, she opened Wahaca in 2008. She now has twelve branches across London.

Bentley's Oyster Bar & Grill **75**.......Late night
Bocca di Lupo **82**........Regular neighbourhood
Le Caprice **76**....................................Late night
Dock Kitchen **61**.........Regular neighbourhood
Dock Kitchen **61**.........Local favourite
Hereford Road **67**......Regular neighbourhood
HIX **84**..Late night
J Sheekey **74**....................................Late night
The Ledbury **67**....................Wish I'd opened
Lucky 7 **67**...Bargain
The River Café **61**......Regular neighbourhood
The River Café **61**.............................High end
Royal China **55**..................................Bargain

CARLO MIRARCHI

Roberta's
261 Moore Street, New York City

Co-owner of runaway Brooklyn hit Roberta's, which opened in 2008 as a no-nonsense, no-reservations, rock 'n' roll bar and pizza joint, and sister establishment Blanca.

St. John Bar and Restaurant **98**......Worth the travel
St. John Bread & Wine **110**....Worth the travel

MARTIN MORALES

Ceviche
17 Frith Street, London

Left Lima at twelve, worked as a Disney Media executive and helped launch iTunes in Europe before opening Peruvian restaurants Ceviche (2012) and Andina (2013) in London.

Bistrot de Luxe **63**....................Local favourite
Burro e Salvia **107**.....Regular neighbourhood
Crab House Café **28**..........................High end
The Ethicurean **34**.................Wish I'd opened
Euro Café **68**....................................Breakfast
Sagar **61**..Bargain
Zhengzhong Lanzhou Lamian **74**.....Late night

JOSH MURPHY

Moon Under Water
211 Gertrude Street, Melbourne

Tasmanian Murphy, head chef and co-owner of the landmark Builders Arms Hotel public house and Moon Under Water, previously headed the kitchen at Cumulus Inc.

Bubbledogs **99**......................Wish I'd opened

SAMUEL NUTTER

Bror
Sankt Peders Stræde 24a, Copenhagen

County Durham-born Nutter opened restaurant Bror ('brother' in Danish) with fellow ex-Noma sous chef and long-time friend Victor Wågman in 2013 to great critical fanfare.

The Raby Hunt Restaurant **28**...........Wish I'd opened

SHUKO ODA

Koya Bar
50 Frith Street, London

Learned the art and hard graft of udon-making at Kunitoraya in Paris, opening London noodle bar Koya in 2010 (recently closed) with John Devitt and Junya Yamasaki, then Koya Bar in 2013.

Dinner by Heston Blumenthal **62**......High end
Franco Manca **92**.......Regular neighbourhood
Silk Road **93**..Bargain
St. John Bread & Wine **110**.....Local favourite

TOM OLDROYD

Polpo
41 Beak Street, London

Oversees all of the restaurants in Russell Norman's rapidly expanding, London-based, Polpo group.

Bar Italia **81**.....................................Late night
Dean Street Townhouse **83**.............Breakfast
Govinda's Pure Vegetarian **84**............Bargain
Quo Vadis **86**.............Regular neighbourhood
St. John Bar and Restaurant **98**.............Local favourite
Tonkotsu **87**....................................Late night
The Wolseley **81**...................Wish I'd opened

RAFAEL OSTERLING

Rafael
San Martin 300, Lima

Left Lima to study and train in Europe, returning to Peru and opening Rafael, where he fuses Peruvian and Mediterranean flavours. Lima's El Mercado and La Despensa in Bogotá followed.

The River Café **61**.................Wish I'd opened

YOTAM OTTOLENGHI
Ottolenghi
287 Upper Street, London
London-based Israeli chef and co-owner
of the eponymous group of sleek Middle East-
ern- Mediterranean deli-cafes with business
partner Sami Tamimi, and Nopi restaurant,
which opened in 2011.
Fernandez & Wells **84**......................Breakfast
Honey & Co. **100**...................Wish I'd opened
Locanda Locatelli **64**.........................High end
Mangal Ocakbasi **97**...........................Bargain
Morito **96**..............................Local favourite
Randall & Aubin **86**.....Regular neighbourhood
Shoryu Ramen **88**............................Late night

NATHAN OUTLAW
Restaurant Nathan Outlaw
St Enodoc Hotel, Rock
Cornish-based seafood specialist, runs
Restaurant Nathan Outlaw and Seafood
& Grill, a variation on the latter opened
in London at The Capital hotel in 2012.
Fresh from the Sea **26**.......................Bargain
Porthminster Café and Restaurant **26**............
Bargain
The Seafood Restaurant **25**...Wish I'd opened
The Seahorse **28**........Regular neighbourhood
The Seahorse **28**.....................Local favourite

PAUL OWENS
The Cliff Restaurant
Derricks, St James
Liverpool-born Owens has lived in Barbados
for twenty-five years, where he now heads
up the kitchen at The Cliff Restaurant.
Le Gavroche **77**.................................High end
Restaurant Gordon Ramsay **57**.........High end

STEVIE PARLE
Dock Kitchen
342–344 Ladbroke Grove, London
Worked at Moro and the River Café,
before opening his own dining room, with
a globetrotting menu, in designer Tom
Dixon's showroom in 2009.
Baiwei **72**...Bargain
Cây Tre **83**..................Regular neighbourhood
The Clove Club **107**..................Local favourite
Dishoom Shoreditch **108**.................Late night
Gymkhana **77**........................Wish I'd opened
Pavilion **102**..................................Breakfast
The River Café **61**.............................High end

TOM PEMBERTON
Hereford Road
3 Hereford Road, London
Driving force behind Hereford Road, which
he opened in West London in 2007 following
his time running St. John Bread & Wine.
The Anchor & Hope **110**.....................Regular
neighbourhood
Dabbous **100**........................Wish I'd opened
Great Queen Street **73**.......................Bargain
The Hand & Flowers **25**........Worth the travel
Moro **96**..Late night
Pied à Terre **100**...............................High end
St. John Bar and Restaurant **98**.............Local
favourite
St. John Bread & Wine **110**..............Breakfast

JOCKY PETRIE
The Ledbury
127 Ledbury Road, London
Resident Scot at The Fat Duck from 2002
to 2013, where he became head of creative
development in 2009, before departing to
become head of development at The Ledbury.
The Hawthorn Restaurant **37**................Worth
the travel
House Café **44**.....................................Bargain
Jackie Lennox Chip Shop **44**............Late night
Tetote Factory **60**.............................Breakfast
The Walpole **60**..................................Bargain

JOSÉ PIZARRO
Pizarro
194 Bermondsey Street, London
Spaniard who's made London his home,
worked with Spanish food purveyors Brindisa
before, in 2011, opening José and Pizarro.
Hutong **92**...................Regular neighbourhood
The India Club **111**.............................Bargain
Murano **79**.......................................High end
Quo Vadis **86**..................................Late night
The Wolseley **81**.............................Breakfast
Zucca **91**..............................Local favourite

BRUCE POOLE
Chez Bruce
2 Bellevue Road, London
Co-owner of Chez Bruce in suburban south-
west London since 1995, he's also a partner
in The Glasshouse and La Trompette.
The Old Spot **34**.......................Local favourite
Red Lion Freehouse **35**.......................Regular
neighbourhood
The Square **80**..................................High end
Sticky Walnut **25**...................Worth the travel
The Walnut Tree **40**...............Worth the travel
The Wolseley **81**.............................Breakfast

ALFRED PRASAD
Tamarind
20 Queen Street, London
Trained at Bukhara and Dum-Pukh, he arrived
at Tamarind in London in 2001, becoming
executive chef for The Tamarind Collection,
which includes Imli Street and Zaika.
Bar Italia **81**....................................Late night
Brindisa Chorizo Grill **92**....................Bargain
Maxim Chinese Restaurant **60**...........Regular
neighbourhood

GLYNN PURNELL

Purnell's
55 Cornwall Street, Birmingham
The loud and proud Brummie did his training under Ramsay, Bosi and Alastair Little before opening the first of his now three establishments in Birmingham in 2007.

Adil **35**....................................Local favourite
Bar Boulud **62**.................................Late night
Cafe Alf Resco **27**............................Breakfast
The Fat Duck **24**................................High end
Al Frash **35**.............................Local favourite
The Hand & Flowers **25**.........Wish I'd opened
Imrans **35**...............................Local favourite
Roka **101**....................Regular neighbourhood

THEO RANDALL

Theo Randall
1 Hamilton Place, London
English cook with an Italian bent, he ran the kitchen at the River Café for over a decade, leaving in 2007 to open Theo Randall at the InterContinental.

Cachao **67**.......................................Breakfast
Lemonia **68**...Bargain
Momo **79**..Late night
La Petite Maison **79**...............Wish I'd opened
Princess Garden of Mayfair **80**...........Regular neighbourhood
The Tangerine Dream Café **58**.................Local favourite
Zuma **63**..High end

NEIL RANKIN

Smokehouse
63–69 Canonbury Road, London
Leaving the realms of fine dining after meeting his mentor Adam Perry Lang, barbeque maestro and ex-Pitt Cue Co. chef Rankin opened Smokehouse in 2013.

Apollo Banana Leaf **69**........................Bargain
The Clove Club **107**...............Wish I'd opened
Duck & Waffle **94**.............................Breakfast
L'Enclume **27**....................Worth the travel
Gymkhana **77**............Regular neighbourhood
Meat Liquor **64**................................Late night
Medlar **57**...High end
The Quality Chop House **96**......Local favourite

SHAUN RANKIN

Ormer
7–11 Don Street, St Helier
A passion for the local produce of his adoptive home of Jersey saw the County Durham-born chef win a Michelin star at his restaurant Ormer just four months after opening.

The Bass & Lobster **36**......................Regular neighbourhood
Green Island Restaurant **36**.....Local favourite
Le Manoir aux Quat'Saisons **32**.........Wish I'd opened
El Tico Beach Cantina **36**.................Breakfast
Zuma **63**..Late night

RENÉ REDZEPI

Noma
Strandgade 93, Copenhagen
Macedonian-Dane behind Noma, opened in 2003, the Nordic-sourced agenda of which has changed haute cuisine in Scandinavia and beyond forever.

The Clove Club **107**...............Worth the travel

ADAM REID

The French by Simon Rogan
The Midland Hotel, Peter Street, Manchester
Manchester born and bred, Reid now runs the kitchen for Simon Rogan at Manchester's century-old Midland Hotel.

Kitchen Table **100**..................Wish I'd opened
Mughli **30**...Late night
The Parlour **29**...........Regular neighbourhood
Sugar Junction **30**...........................Breakfast
The Wharf **30**......................................Bargain
Yang Sing **30**...........................Local favourite

ANDY RICKER

Pok Pok
3226 Southeast Division Street, Portland
Began the Thai-inspired Pok Pok, in Oregon, in 2006, where he also opened Whiskey Soda Lounge, Pok Pok Noi and Sen Yai, followed by three New York outposts.

St. John Bread & Wine **110**....Wish I'd opened

RUTH ROGERS

The River Café
Rainville Road, London
Upstate New York-born co-founder of the River Café, which she opened in West London with the now sadly deceased Rose Gray, in 1987.

Maroush **64**.....................................Late night
St. John Bar and Restaurant **98**.............Local favourite
The Wolseley **81**.............................Breakfast

SHAUN SEARLEY

The Quality Chop House
88–94 Farringdon Road, London
After honing his skills at the Paternoster Chop House and Bistrotheque, Searley assumed cooking duties at the seasonal, ingredient-led Quality Chop House in 2013.

Duck & Waffle **94**............................Late night
The Hand & Flowers **25**....................High end
Kitchen Table **100**..................Wish I'd opened
Pavilion **102**....................................Breakfast
Smokehouse **106**........Regular neighbourhood
St. John Bar and Restaurant **98**.............Local favourite

TOM SELLERS

Restaurant Story
201 Tooley Street, London
Within months of opening Story, at age twenty-six, Sellers received his first Michelin star. The London-based culinary wunderkind trained under luminaries including Thomas Keller, René Redzepi and Tom Aikens.

Dinner by Heston Blumenthal **62**.......High end
The Garrison **90**..............................Breakfast
José **90**.....................Regular neighbourhood
Meat Liquor **64**................................Late night
Meat Liquor **64**...................................Bargain
St. John Bar and Restaurant **98**.............Local favourite

KARAM SETHI
Trishna
15–17 Blandford Street, London
Runs Gymkhana and the British branch of the legendary Mumbai seafood specialist Trishna, having worked at the original outpost, New Delhi's Bukhara and at London's Zuma.

The Delaunay **73**...............................Breakfast
Electric Diner **66**...................Wish I'd opened
Meat Liquor **64**..................................Late night
Patty & Bun **65**......................................Bargain
La Petite Maison **79**..........................High end
Roka **101**....................Regular neighbourhood
Spuntino **87**............................Worth the travel
The Wolseley **81**.......................Local favourite

ILYA SHALEV
Ragout
Bolshaya Gruzinskaya Ulitsa 69, Moscow
A rising star on Moscow's foodie scene, the Israeli chef and co-owner of Ragout restaurant spent eighteen years overseas, under the tutelage of Alain Senderens in Paris among others.

The Ivy **73**..Late night
The Wolseley **81**...............................Breakfast

TIM SIADATAN
Trullo
300–302 St Paul's Road, London
Star graduate of the 2002 first-year intake of Jamie Oliver's Fifteen, he trained further at Moro and St. John, before opening Trullo in 2010.

Le Coq **105**......................................Late night
Le Coq **105**..Bargain
Herman Ze German **111**........Wish I'd opened
Maison d'être **105**...........................Breakfast
Moro **96**..................................Local favourite
The River Café **61**.............................High end
St. John Bread & Wine **110**................Regular neighbourhood

MICHAEL SMITH
The Three Chimneys
1 Colbost, Isle of Skye
A true Highlander who started his career in Inverness, Smith trained in London before returning north to run the much-garlanded Three Chimneys on the Isle of Skye.

Andrew Fairlie **39**..............................High end
Ballinluig Motor Grill **39**.....................Bargain
Citation Taverne & Restaurant **39**.....Breakfast
Loch Bay **37**.............................Local favourite
Moro **96**................................Wish I'd opened
Rocpool **37**.................Regular neighbourhood

CLARE SMYTH
Restaurant Gordon Ramsay
68 Royal Hospital Road, London
Northern Irish, she worked at The Fat Duck, The Waterside Inn, Gidleigh Park and The French Laundry, before joining Restaurant Gordon Ramsay in 2002 and becoming chef-patron in 2013.

Alain Ducasse **75**..............................High end
Bar Boulud **62**...................................Late night
Le Gavroche **77**....................Wish I'd opened
Hibiscus **78**...........................Worth the travel
Scott's **80**....................Regular neighbourhood
Scott's **80**................................Local favourite
Tom's Kitchen **58**............................Breakfast
Zucca **91**..Bargain

BEN SPALDING
Creative Belly Limited
Ran Simon Rogan's two-year London pop-up Roganic in 2011, and after a brief stint at John Salt, launched Creative Belly events, offering experimental pop-up ventures around the UK.

L'Autre Pied **63**........................Local favourite
The Ledbury **67**........................Local favourite
Raj Bari **31**.................Regular neighbourhood
Restaurant Gordon Ramsay **57**..........High end
Street Feast **54**...............................Late night

ADAM STOKES
Adam's
21a Bennett's Hill, Birmingham
Success has come quickly for Lincolnshire-born Stokes: he gained his first Michelin star at twenty-nine, and his eponymous restaurant in Birmingham was awarded the same honour just six months after opening.

Barrafina **82**..........................Wish I'd opened
The Breakfast Club **83**.....................Breakfast
Duck & Waffle **94**...........................Late night
The Ledbury **67**.................................High end
The Malt Shovel **35**.....Regular neighbourhood
Simpsons **35**............................Local favourite
Wee Hurrie **37**....................................Bargain

PEDRO SUBIJANA
Akelarre
Paseo Padre Orcoloaga 56, San Sebastián
One of the founding fathers of New Basque cooking. After training in Madrid, he opened Akelarre in his native San Sebastián in 1975.

The Fat Duck **24**....................Worth the travel

ROBERTA SUDBRACK
Roberta Sudbrack
Rua Lineu Paula Machado 916, Rio de Janeiro
Self-taught, she stood behind the stove at Brazil's presidential palace before opening her Rio restaurant in 2005. In 2012, she designed menus for Brazil's Olympic team.

The River Café **61**..................Worth the travel

AGNAR SVERRISSON
Texture
34 Portman Street, London
Born in Iceland, he worked under Marcus Wareing and Raymond Blanc before launching Texture in 2007.

Busaba Eathai **83**................................Bargain
CUT at 45 Park Lane **76**....................Breakfast
Hakkasan **78**..............Regular neighbourhood
Hakkasan **78**....................................Late night
Le Manoir aux Quat'Saisons **32**.........High end
Zuma **63**................................Wish I'd opened

SAMI TALLBERG

Following a decade in some of the world's most renowned kitchens, Tallberg – an expert on wild food – returned to Helsinki to consult and sell wild plants to Finland's finest restaurants.

Dishoom Shoreditch **108**.....................Regular
neighbourhood

SAMI TAMIMI

Ottolenghi
287 Upper Street, London
Jerusalem-born Tamimi moved to London in 1997 and ran the kitchen at Baker & Spice before joining Yotam Ottolenghi in 2002 to set up their widely acclaimed deli chain.

Abu Zaad **68**..Bargain
Ducksoup **84**...............Regular neighbourhood
Honey & Co. **100**...................Wish I'd opened
KaoSarn **93**......................................Late night
The River Café **61**.............................High end
Sushi Bar Makoto **59**...............Local favourite
The Wolseley **81**..............................Breakfast

KEVIN THORNTON

Thornton's Restaurant
The Fitzwilliam Hotel, Dublin
From County Tipperary, described as 'the great philosopher of Irish food', opened Thornton's in 1995, before transferring his eponymous restaurant to Dublin's Fitzwilliam Hotel in 2002.

Avoca Food Market and Salt Café **48**...Regular
neighbourhood
Kai Café + Restaurant **49**...................Bargain
The Trocadero **47**.....................Local favourite
Vintage Cocktail Club **48**.................Late night

BEN TISH

Salt Yard
54 Goodge Street, London
Launched London tapas concern Salt Yard in 2006. In 2008 he became responsible for overseeing the growing Salt Yard Group, whose latest restaurant is London's Ember Yard.

Antepliler **104**............Regular neighbourhood
Berners Tavern **99**.................Wish I'd opened
Bistrotheque **91**..............................Breakfast
Brasserie Zédel **82**.........................Late night
Delhi Grill **105**..................................Bargain
J Sheekey **74**....................................High end
Rules **74**................................Local favourite

STEPHEN TOMAN

OX
1 Oxford Street, Belfast
Belfast-born Toman opened OX in 2013 with long-standing friend Alain Kerloc'h, whom he met while working at L'Arpège in Paris.

Coppi **41**.....................Regular neighbourhood
Howard Street **41**..............................Bargain
Little Italy **41**.................................Late night
Rayanne House **43**..........................Breakfast
Tedfords **43**.............................Local favourite

MITCH TONKS

The Seahorse
5 South Embankment, Dartmouth
Fishmonger turned restaurateur who runs Bristol's RockFish Grill & Seafood Market, The Seahorse and RockFish Seafood in Dartmouth and Plymouth.

Cafe Alf Resco **27**...........................Breakfast
Crab Shack **28**........................Local favourite
Mayflower **25**............Regular neighbourhood
La Petite Maison **79**..............Wish I'd opened
Rasa Sayang **73**.................................Bargain
Zuma **63**..High end

MICHAEL TOSCANO

Perla
24 Minetta Lane, New York City
Executive chef and co-owner of Perla, Montmartre and Jeffrey's Grocery. Born and raised in Texas, he honed his skills at Mario Batali's Babbo and Manzo.

Fifteen **108**............................Wish I'd opened

MANOJ VASAIKAR

Indian Zing
236 King Street, London
Owner of Indian Zing, Indian Zilla and Indian Zest, Vasaikar was born in Mumbai and moved to London to work at Chutney Mary and Veeraswamy.

Amaya **62**..............................Wish I'd opened
Aqua Shard **91**................................Late night
High Road Brasserie **58**..................Breakfast
HIX **84**...Bargain
La Trompette **59**..........Regular neighbourhood
Sonny's Kitchen **54**.....Regular neighbourhood

EBBE VOLLMER

Vollmers
Tegelgårdsgatan 5, Malmö
Returned to his Swedish hometown of Malmö to open Vollmers in 2011. He's worked in Asia and in the UK with Gordon Ramsay.

L'Atelier de Joël Robuchon **73**............Regular
neighbourhood
Le Manoir aux Quat'Saisons **32**.........Wish I'd
opened

MATS VOLLMER

Vollmers
Tegelgårdsgatan 5, Malmö
Mats and brother Ebbe, the fifth generation of a family of restaurateurs, launched their modern Skåne restaurant in Malmö, a hotbed of culinary attractions, in 2011.

Yauatcha **88**.........................Worth the travel

MARCUS WAREING

Marcus
Wilton Place, London
Re-branded the Gordon Ramsay-operated Petrus as Marcus Wareing at The Berkeley (now called Marcus) in 2008. The Gilbert Scott at London's St. Pancras Renaissance followed in 2011.

Alain Ducasse **75**.............................High end
Bar Boulud **62**.................................Late night
Chez Bruce **70**.......................Local favourite
Colbert **56**.......................................Breakfast
Medlar **57**...................Regular neighbourhood
Scott's **80**..............................Wish I'd opened

PETER WEEDEN

Newman Street Tavern
48 Neman Street, London
Former Paternoster Chop House head chef, he channeled his obsession with provenance into Newman Street Tavern where – as head chef and partner – he serves elegant, fiercely seasonal British fare.

Bone Daddies Ramen Bar **82**...........Late night
Moshi Moshi **94**.........Regular neighbourhood
St. John Bar and Restaurant **98**........Wish I'd
opened
St. John Bread & Wine **110**..............Breakfast
The Quality Chop House **96**................Bargain
The River Café **61**.............................High end
The Sportsman **31**...............Worth the travel
The Wolseley **81**.....................Local favourite

ARJAN WENNEKES

Visaandeschelde
Scheldeplein 4, Amsterdam
Head chef of Visaandeschelde, set in the
heart of Amsterdam and reputed to serve
the best seafood in town, Wennekes previously worked at Klein Paardenburg, ZIN
and Vermeer.
Barbecoa **94**..........................Wish I'd opened

JAMES WILKINS

wilks restaurant
1–3 Chandos Road, Bristol
A glittering career that has taken in stints
at Midsummer House, Aubergine and Michel
Bras was followed in 2012 by the opening in
Bristol of Wilkins's eponymous restaurant,
and in 2014 its first Michelin star.
The Bath Priory Restaurant **33**...............Local
favourite
Le Champignon Sauvage **29**...Worth the travel
The Felin Fach Griffin **40**.....................Regular
neighbourhood

ALYN WILLIAMS

Alyn Williams at the Westbury
The Westbury Hotel, 37 Conduit Street,
London
Londoner Williams spent six years as a
ski-instructor before training with Marcus
Wareing at the Berkeley. His hotel dining
room at the Westbury opened in 2011.
Akash Tandoori **54**..............................Bargain
Brasserie Chavot **76**..............Wish I'd opened
Made in Italy **57**........Regular neighbourhood
Le Manoir aux Quat'Saisons **32**........High end
The Wolseley **81**.............................Breakfast

BRYN WILLIAMS

Odette's
130 Regents Park Road, London
From north Wales, made a name for himself
in 2006 with BBC television's Great British
Menu. He's since revived the long-running
Odette's in London's Primrose Hill.
Benares **75**..High end
Bentley's Oyster Bar & Grill **75**...............Wish
I'd opened
Le Gavroche **77**................................High end
Polpo **85**..Bargain
The Wolseley **81**.......................Local favourite

STEVE WILLIAMS

40 Maltby Street
40 Maltby Street, London
Won The Harwood Arms a Michelin star and
worked at The Ledbury before heading to
Bermondsey to cook up a storm at informal
small-plate wine bar, 40 Maltby Street.
The Anchor & Hope **110**...........Local favourite
The Ledbury **67**................................High end
My Old Place **110**..............................Bargain
Pavilion **102**....................................Breakfast
Ranoush Juice **65**...........................Late night

ED WILSON

Terroirs
5 William IV Street, London
Opened Terroirs in London in 2008, serving
small-plate ingredient-led food and natural
wines, followed by Brawn, Soif and The Green
Man & French Horn.
40 Maltby Street **90**....Regular neighbourhood
The Clove Club **107**...............Wish I'd opened
Embassy East **104**..........................Breakfast
Lucky Chip **101**..................................Bargain
The Quality Chop House **96**......Local favourite
Umut 2000 **98**...............................Late night
The Waterside Inn **24**.......................High end

MARTIN WISHART

Restaurant Martin Wishart
54 The Shore, Edinburgh
Trained in starry kitchens in London and
New York, opening his own restaurant in his
native Edinburgh in 1999. A sister restaurant
in Loch Lomond followed, and an Edinburgh
brasserie.
Hakkasan **78**..................................Late night

JUNYA YAMASAKI

Left Tokyo for Paris, where he swapped Fine
Art studies for the art of noodle-making at
Kunitoraya. Worked at Paris's Rose Bakery
and opened its London branch before open-
ing Koya (2010) and Koya Bar (2013). Has
since closed Koya to return to Japan and
pursue future projects.
Leila's Café **109**...............................Breakfast
The River Café **61**............................High end
Silk Road **93**.....................................Bargain
St. John Bar and Restaurant **98**........Wish I'd
opened
St. John Bread & Wine **110**.................Regular
neighbourhood

RICARDO ZARATE

Mo-Chica
514 West 7th Street, Los Angeles
Lima born, he worked in London at Zuma and
at Pengelly's before moving to Los Angeles to
open the Peruvian-inspired Mo-Chica in 2009,
then Picca (2012) and Paiché (2013).
Nobu **79**................................Worth the travel
Zuma **63**..............................Wish I'd opened

JOCK ZONFRILLO

Orana
285 Rundle Street, Adelaide
Scottish-born Zonfrillo worked his way up
the ranks in London and, seduced by an
antipodean sabbatical, settled in Adelaide,
launching Orana and Street ADL in 2013,
which showcase Australia's indigenous
ingredients.
Dinner by Heston Blumenthal **62**..........Worth
the travel

'Skye seafood straight off the boats'
MICHAEL SMITH P37

'THE BEST FISH AND CHIP SHOP EVER'
ADAM STOKES P37

'STILL THE BEST FINE DINING IN THE UK.'
ISAAC MCHALE P67

UNITED KINGDOM & REPUBLIC OF IRELAND

'WELL WORTH A TRIP INTO THE HIGHLANDS.'
JOCKY PETRIE P37

'CHUNKY CHIPS AND MUSHY PEAS.'
TOM KITCHIN P38

'Beautiful views overlooking the River Lagan.'
STEPHEN TOMAN P43

'WHERE BETTER TO GO LATE AT NIGHT THAN A STREET CALLED "CURRY MILE"?'
ADAM REID P30

THE CROWN AT BRAY

Recommended by
André Garrett

High Street
Bray
Berkshire
England SL6 2AH
+44 1628621936
www.thecrownatbray.com

Opening hours	Open 7 days
Credit cards	Accepted
Price range	Affordable
Style	Casual
Cuisine	Gastropub
Recommended for	Regular neighbourhood

'Lovely, warm, homely pub, with great food from Heston Blumenthal.'—André Garrett

THE FAT DUCK

Recommended by
Sat Bains, Rainer Becker,
Paul Foster, Nigel Haworth,
Tom Kerridge, Glynn
Purnell, Pedro Subijana

High Street
Bray
Berkshire
England SL6 2AQ
+44 1628580333
www.thefatduck.co.uk

Opening hours	Closed Monday and Sunday
Credit cards	Accepted
Price range	Expensive
Style	Smart casual
Cuisine	Modern British
Recommended for	High end

'Heston has created something so innovative and unique at The Fat Duck. It is a meal of sheer joy.' —Rainer Becker

Imaginative, innovative and creative restaurants are ten a penny these days, but for people who want their levels of crazy turned up to eleven there's still only one place to go – even if it's moving to the other side of the planet. From March 2015 The Fat Duck will temporarily relocate to Melbourne, but far from it becoming a pale imitation of his flagship, Heston Blumenthal is moving his entire kitchen brigade Down Under in an attempt to maintain its levels of creativity and sheer brilliance. After six months the iconic snail porridge and 'Mad Hatter fob watch' – along with the chefs – will return to Berkshire and a fully refurbished Fat Duck, while the venue in Oz will continue as a permanent outpost of Dinner by Heston Blumenthal.

THE HINDS HEAD

Recommended by
Tom Kerridge

High Street
Bray
Berkshire
England SL6 2AB
+44 1628626151
www.hindsheadbray.com

Opening hours	Open 7 days
Credit cards	Accepted
Price range	Affordable
Style	Casual
Cuisine	Gastropub
Recommended for	Regular neighbourhood

'Rock-solid, consistent dishes, thoroughly worthy of its Michelin star.'—Tom Kerridge

THE WATERSIDE INN

Recommended by
Galton Blackiston, Dominic
Chapman, Angela
Hartnett, Ed Wilson

Ferry Road
Bray
Berkshire
England SL6 2AT
+44 1628620691
www.waterside-inn.co.uk

Opening hours	Closed Monday and Tuesday
Credit cards	Accepted
Price range	Expensive
Style	Smart casual
Cuisine	French
Recommended for	High end

'Old-fashioned three-star restaurant that all young chefs and front of house should experience to understand the traditional values of restaurateuring.' —Ed Wilson

MAYFLOWER

Recommended by
Mitch Tonks

3a–5 Haymarket Walk
Bristol
England BS1 3LN
+44 1179250555
www.mayflower-bristol.co.uk

Opening hours	Open 7 days
Credit cards	Accepted but not AMEX
Price range	Affordable
Style	Casual
Cuisine	Chinese
Recommended for	Regular neighbourhood

'It's authentic Chinese, only open from 6.00 p.m. to 3.00 a.m. and for dim sum on Sunday. The menu is not typical, lots of offal, great seafood and a strong Chinese clientele – the best Chinese outside of London.'
—Mitch Tonks

CASAMIA

Recommended by
Sat Bains

38 High Street
Westbury-on-Trym
Bristol
England BS9 3DZ
+44 1179592884
www.casamiarestaurant.co.uk

Opening hours	Closed Monday and Sunday
Credit cards	Accepted
Price range	Expensive
Style	Smart casual
Cuisine	Modern British
Recommended for	Worth the travel

THE HAND & FLOWERS

Recommended by
Sat Bains, André Garrett,
Anna Hansen, Tom
Pemberton, Glynn
Purnell, Shaun Searley

126 West Street
Marlow
Buckinghamshire
England SL7 2BP
+44 1628482277
www.thehandandflowers.co.uk

Opening hours	Open 7 days
Credit cards	Accepted
Price range	Affordable
Style	Casual
Cuisine	Gastropub
Recommended for	High end

'Tom has managed to capture the pub, social and comfortable dining atmosphere with outstanding, perfectly executed food. Not over-fussy or trying to be something it's not, just really top food.'—Shaun Searley

STICKY WALNUT

Recommended by
Bruce Poole

11 Charles Street
Chester
Cheshire
England CH2 3AZ
+44 1244400400
www.stickywalnut.com

Opening hours	Open 7 days
Credit cards	Accepted
Price range	Affordable
Style	Casual
Cuisine	British bistro
Recommended for	Worth the travel

'Cracking bistro-type restaurant with bang-on food and a friendly, fun atmosphere.'—Bruce Poole

THE SEAFOOD RESTAURANT

Recommended by
Dominic Chapman,
Nathan Outlaw

Riverside
Padstow
Cornwall
England PL28 8BY
+44 1841532700
www.rickstein.com

Opening hours	Open 7 days
Credit cards	Accepted
Price range	Expensive
Style	Smart casual
Cuisine	Seafood
Recommended for	Wish I'd opened

'It's the perfect fish restaurant in the perfect location.'—Dominic Chapman

FRESH FROM THE SEA

Recommended by
Nathan Outlaw

18 New Road
Port Isaac
Cornwall
England PL29 3SB
+44 1208880849
www.freshfromthesea.co.uk

Opening hours	Open 7 days
Reservation policy	No
Credit cards	Accepted
Price range	Budget
Style	Casual
Cuisine	Seafood
Recommended for	Bargain

'Calum's crabs make a fantastic sandwich and they are fished responsibly too.'—Nathan Outlaw

Perfectly formed little fish shop in the picture-perfect fishing village of Port Isaac on the Atlantic coast of North Cornwall. It is run by the husband-and-wife team Calum and Tracey Greenhalgh, who catch their lobster and crab daily from their own boat, the *Mary D*. They specialize in selling and serving sustainable Cornish fish: from hand-line caught mackerel and pollack, to mussels, oysters and clams from the Camel estuary, and smoked fish from the Tregida Smoke-house. They serve lobster salads and rolls, handpicked crab sandwiches and soup, and their own smoked mackerel pâté with toast.

PORTHMINSTER CAFÉ & RESTAURANT

Recommended by
Nathan Outlaw

Porthminster Beach
St Ives
Cornwall
England TR26 2EB
+44 1736795352
www.porthminstercafe.co.uk

Opening hours	Variable
Credit cards	Accepted
Price range	Affordable
Style	Casual
Cuisine	International
Recommended for	Bargain

'Great food, child friendly and literally right on the beach. What more could you ask for?'—Nathan Outlaw

Sat bang on Porthminster Beach, in the popular Cornish seaside town of St Ives, means getting a table here in season takes a bit of forward planning. Nevertheless, with a handsome modern terrace that overlooks the immaculately clean beach, it's invariably packed throughout the summer due to a menu that understands its audience. Lunch offers simple seafood dishes that take in a few Asian influences, alongside a decent- sized vegetarian section and simple bowls of pasta for the kids. Things get a little more elaborate and expensive in the evening – but not prohibitively so – and the kids will still be alright.

L'ENCLUME

Recommended by
Neil Rankin

Cavendish Street
Cartmel
Cumbria
England LA11 6PZ
+44 1539536362
www.lenclume.co.uk

Opening hours	Open 7 days
Credit cards	Accepted
Price range	Expensive
Style	Smart casual
Cuisine	Modern British
Recommended for	Worth the travel

'There is nobody to touch Simon Rogan's cooking. It's perfectly executed, exciting and modern without being naff. The staff balance that formal/informal line perfectly and the service and food is flawless. The whole "we only source local" and "we grow our own veg" thing can get tiresome sometimes for the punter and is usually badly executed but Simon's team do it with as much of an eye for detail as some of the best growers in the country and it shows. They also do a cracking fry-up the next day.'—Neil Rankin

Thanks to L'Enclume the Lake District can offer greater culinary highlights than twee tea rooms and tourist traps churning out 'hearty' quiches for tired ramblers. Operating out of a former blacksmith's forge since 2006, head chef Simon Rogan was in the vanguard of the now ubiquitous approach of using local ingredients and remains one of the most innovative chefs to have graced the UK restaurant scene in the past decade. Rogan's passion for his produce, seeking out a perplexing variety of unusual herbs and vegetables, isn't yawn-inducingly worthy – nor is it PR puff. Rather, it is driven by a desire to serve decent ingredients in an eye-opening manner.

GIDLEIGH PARK

Recommended by
Shaun Hill

Dartmoor National Park
Chagford
Devon
England TQ13 8HH
+44 1647432367
www.gidleigh.com

Opening hours	Open 7 days
Credit cards	Accepted
Price range	Expensive
Style	Smart casual
Cuisine	Modern European
Recommended for	High end

'I used to work there so can't be relied on for dispassionate appraisal but Caines is an exceptional chef and has stood the test of time.'—Shaun Hill

CAFE ALF RESCO

Recommended by
Glynn Purnell,
Mitch Tonks

Lower Street
Dartmouth
Devon
England TQ6 9AN
+44 1803835880
www.cafealfresco.co.uk

Opening hours	Open 7 days
Reservation policy	No
Credit cards	Not accepted
Price range	Budget
Style	Casual
Cuisine	Café-Bar
Recommended for	Breakfast

'The breakfasts are delicious and just what you need after a night out in the fishing town of Brixham. It is lovely to be able to sit outside and see the sea. Also, once breakfast is done – it's Pimm's o'clock!'
—Glynn Purnell

THE SEAHORSE

Recommended by
Nathan Outlaw

5 South Embankment
Dartmouth
Devon
England TQ6 9BH
+44 1803835147
www.seahorserestaurant.co.uk

Opening hours	Closed Monday
Credit cards	Accepted
Price range	Affordable
Style	Smart casual
Cuisine	Seafood
Recommended for	Local favourite

'It showcases the region's finest ingredients. The food is a reflection of the respect and care that is given to those raw materials.'—Nathan Outlaw

The Devon flagship of accountant turned fishmonger turned self taught chef and restaurateur Mitch Tonks is, it shouldn't surprise you to hear, all about fish. While the smart-looking Seahorse on the bank of the River Dart does cater for carnivores with a couple of dishes under the heading 'Today's Meat', the majority, understandably, come here for the kitchen's way with seafood. Tonks's love of Italy comes across in a menu that features *zuppa del pescatore* (an Italian Riviera fisherman's soup), sea bream *al cartoccio* (steamed in a paper bag) and *fritto misto* of monkfish, soft-shell crab, red mullet, whitebait and squid.

CRAB SHACK

Recommended by
Mitch Tonks

3 Queen Street
Teignmouth
Devon
England TQ14 8BY
+44 1626777956
www.crabshackonthebeach.co.uk

Opening hours	Closed Monday and Tuesday
Credit cards	Accepted
Price range	Affordable
Style	Casual
Cuisine	Seafood
Recommended for	Local favourite

'It's run by Rob Simmonds, a crab fisherman and his wife, Amanda, and they serve the area's best shellfish with a big emphasis on crab and lobster. We have the best seafood in the world down here and it's worth travelling for; it never tastes as good in the middle of a city.'—Mitch Tonks

HIX OYSTER & FISH HOUSE

Recommended by
Margot Henderson

Cobb Road
Lyme Regis
Dorset
England DT7 3JP
+44 1297446910
www.hixoysterandfishhouse.co.uk

Opening hours	Variable
Credit cards	Accepted
Price range	Affordable
Style	Smart casual
Cuisine	Seafood
Recommended for	Worth the travel

CRAB HOUSE CAFÉ

Recommended by
Martin Morales

Ferrymans Way
Wyke Regis
Dorset
England DT4 9YU
+44 1305788867
www.crabhousecafe.co.uk

Opening hours	Closed Monday and Tuesday
Credit cards	Accepted
Price range	Affordable
Style	Casual
Cuisine	Seafood
Recommended for	High end

'It's neither high end, nor expensive, but I love to go there on special occasions. Exceptional, freshly caught seafood is on offer, simply cooked and set in a beautiful location.'—Martin Morales

THE RABY HUNT RESTAURANT

Recommended by
Samuel Nutter

The Raby Hunt Inn
Summerhouse
Near Darlington
Co. Durham
England DL2 3UD
+44 1325374237
www.rabyhuntrestaurant.co.uk

Opening hours	Closed Sunday to Tuesday
Credit cards	Accepted
Price range	Expensive
Style	Smart casual
Cuisine	British
Recommended for	Wish I'd opened

'This restaurant is located close to where I grew up in the northeast of England. I had always dreamed of having a restaurant in this very rural area, but always feared that it would not be a success. The head chef and proprietor, James Close, had the guts to do it and has such a fantastic restaurant that has achieved and maintained its first Michelin star.'—Samuel Nutter

THE LANDGATE BISTRO

Recommended by
Timothy Johnson

5–6 Landgate
Rye
East Sussex
England TN31 7LH
+44 1797222829
www.landgatebistro.co.uk

Opening hours	Closed Monday and Tuesday
Credit cards	Accepted
Price range	Affordable
Style	Casual
Cuisine	British
Recommended for	Regular neighbourhood

'Local food cooked simply.'—Timothy Johnson

THE COMPANY SHED

Recommended by
Miles Kirby

129 Coast Road
West Mersea
Essex
England CO5 8PA
+44 1206382700
www.the-company-shed.co.uk

Opening hours	Closed Monday
Reservation policy	No
Credit cards	Not accepted
Price range	Budget
Style	Casual
Cuisine	Seafood
Recommended for	Worth the travel

A weather-beaten hut among the boatyards of West Mersea on the Essex coast, The Company Shed is a quirky fishmonger's with a few tables. Opened in the late 1980s by Heather Haward, originally as a weekend-only concern to sell husband Richard's fish and oysters, it's gained a cult following. The combination of setting, BYOB and the honest pleasures of smoked fish, dressed crab and simply grilled shellfish are irresistible to anyone with a love of seafood and salty air. Make the journey September to April to try the local native oysters that get their distinctive green hue and flavour from the salt marshes.

LE CHAMPIGNON SAUVAGE

Recommended by
James Wilkins

24–26 Suffolk Road
Cheltenham
Gloucestershire
England GL50 2AQ
+44 1242573449
www.lechampignonsauvage.co.uk

Opening hours	Closed Monday and Sunday
Credit cards	Accepted
Price range	Affordable
Style	Smart casual
Cuisine	Modern French
Recommended for	Worth the travel

'Great all-round restaurant experience from two very experienced people. Refreshing to be looked after by people who know what they are doing and who are not chasing trends.'—James Wilkins

THE PARLOUR

Recommended by
Adam Reid

60 Beech Road
Chorlton
Greater Manchester
England M21 9EG
+44 1618814871
www.theparlour.info

Opening hours	Open 7 days
Credit cards	Accepted
Price range	Affordable
Style	Casual
Cuisine	Gastropub
Recommended for	Regular neighbourhood

'The Parlour shows how Manchester is growing to envelop the suburbs. It does quirky pub food at a good price in a lively and fuss-free style.'—Adam Reid

MUGHLI

Recommended by
Adam Reid

30 Wilmslow Road
Manchester
Greater Manchester
England M14 5TQ
+44 1612480900
www.mughli.com

Opening hours	Open 7 days
Credit cards	Accepted
Price range	Budget
Style	Casual
Cuisine	Indian-Pakistani
Recommended for	Late night

'Where better to go late at night than a street called "Curry Mile"? Mughli provide great food even after I have had a late finish in the kitchen.'—Adam Reid

SUGAR JUNCTION

Recommended by
Adam Reid

60 Tib Street
Manchester
Greater Manchester
England M4 1LG
+44 1618391444
www.sugarjunction.co.uk

Opening hours	Open 7 days
Credit cards	Accepted
Price range	Budget
Style	Casual
Cuisine	Café-Bar-Bistro
Recommended for	Breakfast

'It's in the Northern Quarter and offers simple but hearty breakfasts with good coffee. With its charming 1950s-style theme, it's a great way to start the weekend.'—Adam Reid

THE WHARF

Recommended by
Adam Reid

6 Slate Wharf
Manchester
Greater Manchester
England M15 4SW
+44 1612202960
www.brunningandprice.co.uk/thewharf

Opening hours	Open 7 days
Credit cards	Accepted but not AMEX
Price range	Affordable
Style	Casual
Cuisine	Gastropub
Recommended for	Bargain

'A Brunning and Price pub gives you tasty, affordable food and a good pint as well.'—Adam Reid

YANG SING

Recommended by
Adam Reid

34 Princess Street
Manchester
Greater Manchester
England M1 4JY
+44 1612362200
www.yang-sing.com

Opening hours	Open 7 days
Credit cards	Accepted
Price range	Affordable
Style	Casual
Cuisine	Cantonese
Recommended for	Local favourite

'It might be a big place nowadays but it serves great-quality, tasty food and sums up the ethnic diversity that Manchester offers.'—Adam Reid

THE BLACK RAT RESTAURANT

Recommended by
Tom Adams

88 Chesil Street
Winchester
Hampshire
England SO23 0HX
+44 1962844465
www.theblackrat.co.uk

Opening hours	Open 7 days
Credit cards	Accepted
Price range	Affordable
Style	Smart casual
Cuisine	Modern British
Recommended for	Wish I'd opened

'Beautiful space and beautiful food. They make it feel so effortless, which it is not.'—Tom Adams

THE GOODS SHED RESTAURANT

Recommended by
Stephen Harris

Station Road West
Canterbury
Kent
England CT2 8AN
+44 1227459153
www.thegoodsshed.co.uk

Opening hours	Closed Monday
Credit cards	Accepted
Price range	Affordable
Style	Casual
Cuisine	British bistro
Recommended for	Local favourite

THE SPORTSMAN

Faversham Road
Seasalter
Kent
England CT5 4BP
+44 1227273370
www.thesportsmanseasalter.co.uk

Recommended by
Adam Byatt, Kobe
Desramaults, Mike
Eggert, Henry Harris,
Angela Hartnett,
Peter Weeden

Opening hours	Closed Monday
Credit cards	Accepted
Price range	Affordable
Style	Casual
Cuisine	Gastropub
Recommended for	Worth the travel

'A pub in the middle of nowhere that makes its own butter and you can see the vegetables that they use growing outside and the lambs in the field destined for your plate. The food that is cooked shows a love of craft.'—Henry Harris

What chef-proprietor Stephen Harris likes to describe as a 'grotty rundown pub by the sea' is exactly what The Sportsman was before he took it over in 1999. Today, despite its somewhat desolate location, 3 km (2 miles) outside Whitstable on the Kent coast, it has become a destination, a place of gastronomic pilgrimage based purely on the quality of its cooking. There are two menus – the daily-changing à la carte and a tasting menu that has to be ordered at least forty-eight hours in advance, and for which you'd be advised to put your name down for when you book.

RAJ BARI

6–7 Tubs Hill Parade
Sevenoaks
Kent
England TN13 1DH
+44 1732743315
www.rajbari.co.uk

Recommended by
Ben Spalding

Opening hours	Open 7 days
Credit cards	Accepted but not AMEX
Price range	Budget
Style	Casual
Cuisine	Indian
Recommended for	Regular neighbourhood

'Immaculate Indian food served with style, playfulness and theatre, with well-drilled and equally immaculate waiters. Passion shines through and they just get how to look after the customer.'—Ben Spalding

THE PLEASANT CAFÉ

7 Mount Pleasant Road
Tunbridge Wells
Kent
England TN1 1NT
+44 1892518632

Recommended by
Timothy Johnson

Opening hours	Open 7 days
Reservation policy	No
Credit cards	Not accepted
Price range	Budget
Style	Casual
Cuisine	Café
Recommended for	Breakfast

'For a full English breakfast and a couple of hours of reading.'—Timothy Johnson

DAVID BROWN DELICATESSEN

28a Harbour Street
Whitstable
Kent
England CT5 1DB
+44 1227274507

Recommended by
Stephen Harris

Opening hours	Open 7 days
Credit cards	Accepted but not AMEX
Price range	Budget
Style	Casual
Cuisine	Mediterranean
Recommended for	Regular neighbourhood

ELLIOTT'S COFFEE SHOP

1 Harbour Street
Whitstable
Kent
England CT5 1AG
+44 1227276608

Recommended by
Stephen Harris

Opening hours	Open 7 days
Credit cards	Accepted
Price range	Budget
Style	Casual
Cuisine	Café-Bistro
Recommended for	Breakfast

CLAYTON STREET CHIPPY

Recommended by
Nigel Haworth

9 Clayton Street
Blackburn
Lancashire
England BB6 7AQ

Opening hours	Open 7 days
Reservation policy	No
Credit cards	Not accepted
Price range	Budget
Style	Casual
Cuisine	Fish and Chips
Recommended for	Bargain

THE INN AT WHITEWELL

Recommended by
Nigel Haworth

Whitewell
Forest of Bowland
Lancashire
England BB7 3AT
+44 1200448222
www.innatwhitewell.com

Opening hours	Open 7 days
Credit cards	Accepted
Price range	Affordable
Style	Casual
Cuisine	British
Recommended for	Local favourite

RESTAURANT SAT BAINS

Recommended by
Jason Atherton,
Michael Meredith

Lenton Lane
Nottingham
Nottinghamshire
England NG7 2SA
+44 1159866566
www.restaurantsatbains.com

Opening hours	Closed Monday and Sunday
Credit cards	Accepted
Price range	Expensive
Style	Smart casual
Cuisine	Modern British
Recommended for	Worth the travel

One of the UK's most gastronomically adventurous destination restaurants is unconventionally set on the industrial outskirts of Nottingham. A modern take on the old-fashioned concept of the husband-and-wife-run restaurant with rooms, Sat and Amanda Bains's edgily located, urban oasis is housed in a collection of renovated Victorian farm buildings that predate the panorama of pylons. Book a night in one of the eight rooms plus dinner at either the chef's or the kitchen table – the former overlooking the main kitchen, the latter with your own personal chef – to get closer to the cutting-edge but playful cooking.

LE MANOIR AUX QUAT'SAISONS

Recommended by
Jeff Galvin, Shaun
Rankin, Agnar
Sverrisson, Ebbe
Vollmer, Alyn Williams

Church Road
Great Milton
Oxfordshire
England OX44 7PD
+44 1844278881
www.manoir.com

Opening hours	Open 7 days
Credit cards	Accepted
Price range	Expensive
Style	Smart casual
Cuisine	Modern French
Recommended for	Wish I'd opened

'It's one of Britain's greatest culinary experiences and a truly luxurious place. Any chef would be envious of the extensive kitchen gardens. It's an obvious labour of love for Raymond Blanc and a great success for him.'
—Shaun Rankin

SHAUN DICKENS AT THE BOATHOUSE
Recommended by
Raymond Blanc

Station Road
Henley-on-Thames
Oxfordshire
England RG9 1AZ
+44 1491577937
www.shaundickens.co.uk

Opening hours	Closed Monday
Credit cards	Accepted
Price range	Affordable
Style	Smart casual
Cuisine	Modern European
Recommended for	Local favourite

'I love Shaun's food – the dishes are simple, they do not use too many ingredients, yet the ones chosen are perfectly matched so the flavours are incredible. Shaun is hugely passionate about seasonality and using the very best local produce and he spends so much time selecting his suppliers.'—Raymond Blanc

THE BATH PRIORY RESTAURANT
Recommended by
James Wilkins

The Bath Priory
Weston Road
Bath
Somerset
England BA1 2XT
+44 1225331922
www.thebathpriory.co.uk

Opening hours	Open 7 days
Credit cards	Accepted
Price range	Expensive
Style	Formal
Cuisine	Modern European
Recommended for	Local favourite

'Stunning gardens in the summer and a good-value lunch menu.'—James Wilkins

THE EASTERN EYE
Recommended by
Hywel Jones

8a Quiet Street
Bath
Somerset
England BA1 2JS
+44 1225422323
www.easterneye.com

Opening hours	Open 7 days
Credit cards	Accepted
Price range	Affordable
Style	Casual
Cuisine	Bengali
Recommended for	Late night

'Brilliant Indian restaurant in the centre of Bath, with a stunning dining room, extremely accommodating staff (even for a late-night table of chefs!) and most importantly, great food. Ask them to create you a bespoke menu and you won't be disappointed.' —Hywel Jones

JIKA JIKA
Recommended by
Hywel Jones

4 Brunel Square
Bath
Somerset
England BA1 1SX
+44 1225469253
www.jikajika.co.uk

Opening hours	Open 7 days
Credit cards	Accepted but not AMEX
Price range	Budget
Style	Casual
Cuisine	Café-Bistro
Recommended for	Breakfast

'Fantastic coffee and simple but great-quality food specializing in the West Country's finest produce. A must-visit place if ever I'm in the city centre early in the morning.'—Hywel Jones

THE OLD SPOT

Recommended by
Bruce Poole

12 Sadler Street
Wells
Somerset
England BA5 2SE
+44 1749689099
www.theoldspot.co.uk

Opening hours	Closed Monday
Credit cards	Accepted
Price range	Affordable
Style	Casual
Cuisine	European
Recommended for	Local favourite

'Wonderfully classical and intelligent food with
a great wine list, overlooking beautiful Wells Cathedral.
What's not to like? I wish I had a place of this quality
near where I live!'—Bruce Poole

THE ETHICUREAN

Recommended by
Martin Morales

Barley Wood Walled Garden
Long Lane
Wrington
Somerset
England BS40 5SA
+44 1934863713
www.theethicurean.com

Opening hours	Closed Monday
Credit cards	Accepted
Price range	Affordable
Style	Casual
Cuisine	Modern British
Recommended for	Wish I'd opened

'The Ethicurean team are not just a lovely bunch of
guys, they also create some of the most imaginative
dishes and drinks from produce gathered no further
than one mile from their restaurant. They grow much
of what they cook; they forage, hunt, pickle or smoke
their produce before artistically displaying it on dishes.
The setting is also stunning – set in a walled garden
on one side of a valley, it has some of the most
spectacular sunsets anywhere in the world.'
—Martin Morales

PEA PORRIDGE

Recommended by
Paul Foster

28–29 Cannon Street
Bury St Edmunds
Suffolk
England IP33 1JR
+44 1284700200
www.peaporridge.co.uk

Opening hours	Closed Monday and Sunday
Credit cards	Accepted but not AMEX
Price range	Affordable
Style	Casual
Cuisine	European
Recommended for	Local favourite

'Solid cooking and full-on flavours. Uncomplicated,
tasty food with a maximum of four components per
plate.'—Paul Foster

The cosmopolitan cooking comes as quite a surprise
at this bijou restaurant, set on a quiet backstreet of
a handsome market town. The interior is all English
country cottage – stripped wooden floors, pine
furniture, an open fire – while the menu gallops
gaily from the Middle East, across Spain, France and
North Africa, touting the likes of pimentón-infused
braised octopus, or Tuscan-style pig's cheeks with
polenta. In-the-know locals love the great-value set
menus (£16.95 for three courses). Service is as
charming as the setting, and the wine list cut from
Old World artisan growers. Stop for a pre-dinner
drink at The Old Cannon Brewery across the road.

HOO HING SUPERMARKET

Recommended by
Ollie Couillaud

Bond Road
Mitcham
Surrey
England CR4 3EB
+44 2086872633
www.hoohing.com

Opening hours	Open 7 days
Reservation policy	No
Credit cards	Accepted
Price range	Budget
Style	Casual
Cuisine	Chinese
Recommended for	Bargain

'The canteen is inside Hoo Hing Chinese supermarket.
They do the most delish food at ridiculously cheap
prices.'—Ollie Couillaud

THE MALT SHOVEL

Barston Lane
Barston
West Midlands
England B92 0JP
+44 1675443223
www.themaltshovelatbarston.com

Opening hours	Open 7 days
Credit cards	Accepted
Price range	Affordable
Style	Casual
Cuisine	Gastropub
Recommended for	Regular neighbourhood

'Good-quality, affordable dining and always consistent.'
—Adam Stokes

ADIL

148–150 Stoney Lane
Birmingham
West Midlands
England B12 8AJ
+44 1214490335
www.adilbalti.co.uk

Opening hours	Open 7 days
Credit cards	Accepted
Price range	Affordable
Style	Casual
Cuisine	Indian-Pakistani
Recommended for	Local favourite

AL FRASH

186 Ladypool Road
Birmingham
West Midlands
England B12 8JS
+44 1217533120
www.alfrash.com

Opening hours	Open 7 days
Credit cards	Accepted
Price range	Budget
Style	Casual
Cuisine	Indian-Pakistani
Recommended for	Local favourite

'Birmingham is well known for its curry culture. The
Balti Triangle – the area established in the mid-1970s
by the Pakistani and Kasmiri communities – really
represents the multicultural flavours of my city!'
—Glynn Purnell

IMRANS

262–266 Ladypool Road
Birmingham
West Midlands
England B12 8JU
+44 1214491370
www.imrans.com

Opening hours	Open 7 days
Credit cards	Accepted
Price range	Budget
Style	Casual
Cuisine	Indian-Pakistani
Recommended for	Local favourite

SIMPSONS

20 Highfield Road
Birmingham
West Midlands
England B15 3DU
+44 1214543434
www.simpsonsrestaurant.co.uk

Opening hours	Open 7 days
Credit cards	Accepted
Price range	Expensive
Style	Smart casual
Cuisine	Modern British
Recommended for	Local favourite

'Andreas Antona is the godfather of Birmingham
cooking.'—Adam Stokes

RED LION FREEHOUSE

East Chisenbury
Pewsey
Wiltshire
England SN9 6AQ
+44 1980671124
www.redlionfreehouse.com

Opening hours	Open 7 days
Credit cards	Accepted but not AMEX
Price range	Affordable
Style	Casual
Cuisine	Gastropub
Recommended for	Regular neighbourhood

'Fantastic food and lovely hospitality in a proper pub.
It's a gem.'—Bruce Poole

GREEN ISLAND RESTAURANT

Recommended by
Shaun Rankin

Green Island
St Clement
Jersey
Channel Islands JE2 6LS
+44 1534857787
www.greenisland.je

Opening hours	Closed Monday
Credit cards	Accepted
Price range	Affordable
Style	Casual
Cuisine	Mediterranean
Recommended for	Local favourite

'They do a fantastic seafood plate that has to be enjoyed leisurely on the terrace with a chilled bottle of Sancerre.'—Shaun Rankin

SIAM GARDEN

Recommended by
Mark Jordan

6 Parade Arcade
St Helier
Jersey
Channel Islands JE2 3QP
+44 1534766776
www.siamgardenjersey.com

Opening hours	Open 7 days
Credit cards	Accepted
Price range	Budget
Style	Casual
Cuisine	Thai
Recommended for	Regular neighbourhood

'This fantastic little Thai restaurant is run by some Thai women and they do the best Thai food that I have ever tasted. Everything is made fresh to order and to original recipes.'—Mark Jordan

THE BASS & LOBSTER

Recommended by
Shaun Rankin

Gorey Coast Road
St Martin
Jersey
Channel Islands JE3 6EU
+44 1534859590
www.bassandlobster.com

Opening hours	Closed Monday
Credit cards	Accepted
Price range	Affordable
Style	Casual
Cuisine	Seafood
Recommended for	Regular neighbourhood

'I have two small children, which can be a handful at times, so it's important to feel comfortable when out dining as a family and know that nothing is a problem. The service coupled with great, honest food ticks all of the boxes for our family.'—Shaun Rankin

BIG VERN'S

Recommended by
Mark Jordan

La Grande Route des Mielles
St Ouen
Jersey
Channel Islands JE3 7FN
+44 1534481705

Opening hours	Open 7 days
Reservation policy	No
Credit cards	Accepted but not AMEX
Price range	Affordable
Style	Casual
Cuisine	Diner-Café
Recommended for	Breakfast

'My favourite place to go for breakfast has to be Big Vern's down alongside the five-mile beach on St Ouen's Bay. It's a café right on the beach and they make an awesome breakfast. I love the feel of the restaurant, it's very rustic with surf pictures on the walls and has a really relaxed, surfy style about it. My kids love it there.'—Mark Jordan

EL TICO BEACH CANTINA

Recommended by
Shaun Rankin

La Grande Route des Mielles
St Ouen
Jersey
Channel Islands JE3 7FN
+44 1534482009
www.elticojersey.com

Opening hours	Open 7 days
Credit cards	Accepted
Price range	Affordable
Style	Casual
Cuisine	International
Recommended for	Breakfast

'I can tuck into a smoky bacon roll while the kids enjoy stacks of Yankee Pancakes with mascarpone cream and maple syrup. The standout feature of this cantina is the breathtaking view over the long stretch of St Ouen's Bay – the perfect spot for a bracing sea walk after all that breakfast.'—Shaun Rankin

THE HAWTHORN RESTAURANT

Recommended by
Jocky Petrie

5 Keil Crofts
Benderloch
Argyll
Scotland PA37 1QS
+44 1631720777

Opening hours	Closed Monday
Credit cards	Accepted but not AMEX
Price range	Affordable
Style	Casual
Cuisine	British
Recommended for	Worth the travel

'This small husband-and-wife-run restaurant is well worth a trip into the Highlands.'—Jocky Petrie

WEE HURRIE

Recommended by
Adam Stokes

Troon Harbour
Troon
Ayrshire
Scotland KA10 6DH

Opening hours	Closed Monday
Reservation policy	No
Credit cards	Not accepted
Price range	Budget
Style	Casual
Cuisine	Fish and Chips
Recommended for	Bargain

'The best fish-and-chip shop ever and it's next to a wholesale fish market in a harbour.'—Adam Stokes

ROCPOOL

Recommended by
Michael Smith

1 Ness Walk
Inverness
County of Inverness
Scotland IV3 5NE
+44 1463717274
www.rocpoolrestaurant.com

Opening hours	Closed Sunday
Credit cards	Accepted
Price range	Affordable
Style	Casual
Cuisine	Brasserie
Recommended for	Regular neighbourhood

'Consistently delivers delicious food. Steven, the owner, is always there, leading from the front and welcoming regulars, families and tourists alike with typical Highland charm.'—Michael Smith

LOCH BAY

Recommended by
Michael Smith

Stein
Isle of Skye
County of Inverness
Scotland IV55 8GA
+44 1470592235
www.lochbay-seafood-restaurant.co.uk

Opening hours	Closed Sunday to Tuesday
Credit cards	Accepted
Price range	Affordable
Style	Casual
Cuisine	Seafood
Recommended for	Local favourite

'Skye seafood straight off the boats, cooked simply.'
—Michael Smith

THE KITCHIN

Recommended by
Neil Borthwick

78 Commercial Quay
Edinburgh
Scotland EH6 6LX
+44 1315551755
www.thekitchin.com

Opening hours	Closed Monday and Sunday
Credit cards	Accepted
Price range	Expensive
Style	Smart casual
Cuisine	Modern Scottish
Recommended for	Worth the travel

'I admire the from-nature-to-plate philosophy. Tom has a real passion for Scottish ingredients and it shows.'
—Neil Borthwick

ONDINE RESTAURANT

Recommended by
Tom Kitchin

2 George IV Bridge
Edinburgh
Scotland EH1 1AD
+44 1312261888
www.ondinerestaurant.co.uk

Opening hours	Closed Sunday
Credit cards	Accepted
Price range	Affordable
Style	Casual
Cuisine	Seafood
Recommended for	Local favourite

'Edinburgh's food scene is brilliant at the moment. It's amazing to see chefs making the most of the high-quality produce available right on our doorstep. Roy Brett's restaurant Ondine, off the Royal Mile, is one of my favourites in Edinburgh. The shellfish is of fantastic quality and I especially like Roy's commitment to sustainable Scottish fish and shellfish.'—Tom Kitchin

URBAN ANGEL

Recommended by
Tom Kitchin

121 Hanover Street
Edinburgh
Scotland EH2 1DJ
+44 1312256215
www.urban-angel.co.uk

Opening hours	Open 7 days
Credit cards	Accepted but not AMEX
Price range	Budget
Style	Casual
Cuisine	Café-Bistro
Recommended for	Breakfast

'It's a little gem for breakfast! They do delicious scrambled eggs and freshly made artisan bread.'
—Tom Kitchin

ANSTRUTHER FISH BAR

Recommended by
Tom Kitchin

42–44 Shore Anstruther
Fife
Scotland KY10 3AQ
+44 1333310518
www.anstrutherfishbar.co.uk

Opening hours	Open 7 days
Reservation policy	No
Credit cards	Accepted but not AMEX
Price range	Budget
Style	Casual
Cuisine	Fish and Chips
Recommended for	Bargain

'The family-run Anstruther Fish Bar is situated in a small fishing village in Fife. Their fish is caught fresh every day from the local quayside and they serve it traditionally with chunky chips and mushy peas. Something I love to do when I can is get together with family and friends and head outside of Edinburgh city centre. Whenever I do, I always make a stop at Anstruther – there's nothing better than enjoying the views over the bay with a delicious fish supper.'
—Tom Kitchin

THE PEAT INN

Recommended by
Tom Kitchin

On the B940
near St Andrews
Fife
Scotland KY15 5LH
+44 1334840206
www.thepeatinn.co.uk

Opening hours	Closed Monday and Sunday
Credit cards	Accepted
Price range	Affordable
Style	Smart casual
Cuisine	Scottish
Recommended for	High end

'I love The Peat Inn. Geoffrey Smeddle and his wife, Katherine, do a fantastic job up there and the food is always first class.'—Tom Kitchin

CITATION TAVERNE & RESTAURANT

Michael Smith

40 Wilson Glasgow
Glasgow
Scotland G1 1HD
+44 1415596799
www.citation-glasgow.com

Opening hours	Open 7 days
Credit cards	Accepted
Price range	Affordable
Style	Casual
Cuisine	British bistro
Recommended for	Breakfast

'Order their Full Écosse and you won't need to eat again for the entire day!'—Michael Smith

ANDREW FAIRLIE

Recommended by
Michael Smith

Gleneagles Hotel
Auchterarder
Perthshire
Scotland PH3 1NF
+44 1764694267
www.andrewfairlie.co.uk

Opening hours	Closed Sunday
Credit cards	Accepted
Price range	Expensive
Style	Smart casual
Cuisine	Modern French
Recommended for	High end

'Luxury in a relaxed atmosphere.'—Michael Smith

BALLINLUIG MOTOR GRILL

Recommended by
Michael Smith

Ballinluig Services, A9
Ballinluig
Perthshire
Scotland PH9 0LG
+44 1796482212
www.ballinluigservices.co.uk

Opening hours	Open 7 days
Reservation policy	No
Credit cards	Accepted but not AMEX
Price range	Budget
Style	Casual
Cuisine	British
Recommended for	Bargain

'When travelling to Edinburgh or Glasgow I always stop at this authentic "truckers" diner for sausage, egg and chips served by local ladies in tabards.'—Michael Smith

THE HARBOURMASTER

Recommended by
Hywel Jones

Harbourmaster Hotel
Pen Cei
Aberaeron
Ceredigion
Wales SA46 0BT
+44 1545570755
www.harbour-master.com

Opening hours	Open 7 days
Credit cards	Accepted
Price range	Affordable
Style	Casual
Cuisine	British
Recommended for	Wish I'd opened

'A truly stunning location on the harbour's edge in Aberaeron. Over the past decade it's developed into a national icon. A thriving business built on great Welsh food and true Welsh hospitality.'—Hywel Jones

THE HARDWICK

Recommended by
Shaun Hill, Hywel Jones

Old Raglan Road
Abergavenny
Monmouthshire
Wales NP7 9AA
+44 1873854220
www.thehardwick.co.uk

Opening hours	Open 7 days
Credit cards	Accepted
Price range	Affordable
Style	Casual
Cuisine	British
Recommended for	Local favourite

'Wales is fortunate to have a chef of Stephen Terry's calibre plying his trade there and flying the flag for Welsh produce with such clear passion. A restaurant that suits all occasions and an extremely family friendly one too.'—Hywel Jones

A London-restaurant-scene legend, chef Stephen Terry returned to his native Wales to take ownership of a pub called the Horse & Jockey on the outskirts of Abergavenny, the Monmouthshire market town famous for the Walnut Tree and the annual food festival it hosts each September. Reopened as The Hardwick four weeks after he first took it over in 2005, it has since grown into an award-winning restaurant with rooms. Terry's unfussy menu makes the most of the best local ingredients, combining them with the good taste and technical ability with which he originally made his name.

THE WALNUT TREE

Recommended by
Jacob Kenedy,
Bruce Poole

Llanddewi Skirrid
Abergavenny
Monmouthshire
Wales NP7 8AW
+44 1873852797
www.thewalnuttreeinn.com

Opening hours	Closed Monday and Sunday
Credit cards	Accepted but not AMEX
Price range	Affordable
Style	Casual
Cuisine	Modern British
Recommended for	Worth the travel

'Shaun Hill has more nous than most in my game and a philosophy we can all aspire to.'—Jacob Kenedy

One of the Britain's great cooking heroes, Shaun Hill 'retired' to Abergavenny to take over The Walnut Tree in 2007. He formerly ran the fine and tiny Merchant House in Ludlow, where he always cooked alone. He has more help in the kitchen here, a famous dining destination on and off since the 1960s. The cooking, wonderfully straightforward but with the sort of seasoned skill that only years at the stove can bring, makes use of local produce sourced from Monmouth-shire's rich larder. Make a proper meal of it and book a room in one of their two nearby cottages.

THE FELIN FACH GRIFFIN

Recommended by
James Wilkins

Felin Fach
Brecon
Powys
Wales LD3 0UB
+44 1874620111
www.felinfachgriffin.co.uk

Opening hours	Open 7 days
Credit cards	Accepted but not AMEX
Price range	Affordable
Style	Casual
Cuisine	Gastropub
Recommended for	Regular neighbourhood

'I love to go walking on the Brecon Beacons and this place is the perfect welcoming country pub with a log fire, good beers and good food.'—James Wilkins

THE FIG TREE

Recommended by
Hywel Jones

The Esplanade
Penarth
Vale of Glamorgan
Wales CF64 3AU
+44 2920702512
www.thefigtreepenarth.co.uk

Opening hours	Closed Monday
Credit cards	Accepted but not AMEX
Price range	Affordable
Style	Casual
Cuisine	British
Recommended for	Regular neighbourhood

'A great neighbourhood restaurant run by Mike Caplain and Sandy Guppy. Fantastic seaside location, great food, service and value with a refreshingly large vegetarian offering on the menu. '—Hywel Jones

CANTEEN AT THE MAC

Recommended by
Niall McKenna

Metropolitan Arts Centre
10 Exchange Street West
Belfast
County Antrim
Northern Ireland BT1 2NJ
+44 2890235053
www.themaclive.com

Opening hours	Open 7 days
Credit cards	Accepted but not AMEX
Price range	Affordable
Style	Casual
Cuisine	Café-Bistro
Recommended for	Breakfast

'Great on a Sunday morning with the papers and the kids can have a wander around. I love the ambience of the place – it is open, cleverly designed with gallery spaces and there is always a relaxed vibe.'
—Niall McKenna

COPPI

St Anne's Square
Belfast
County Antrim
Northern Ireland BT1 2LR
+44 2890311959
www.coppi.co.uk

Recommended by
Stephen Toman

Opening hours	Open 7 days
Credit cards	Accepted
Price range	Affordable
Style	Casual
Cuisine	Italian Bistro
Recommended for	Regular neighbourhood

'Chilled-out vibe in beautiful surroundings, great for a Sunday evening.'—Stephen Toman

THE GREAT ROOM RESTAURANT

The Merchant Hotel
16 Skipper Street
Belfast
County Antrim
Northern Ireland BT1 2DZ
+44 2890234888
www.themerchanthotel.com

Recommended by
Niall McKenna

Opening hours	Open 7 days
Credit cards	Accepted
Price range	Affordable
Style	Smart casual
Cuisine	Brasserie
Recommended for	High end

'To be honest it is hard to beat the Champagne high tea at The Merchant Hotel. The building and dining room are truly breathtaking and the afternoon tea is classic. The drinks, service and atmosphere at their award-winning cocktail bar are second to none.'
—Niall McKenna

HOWARD STREET

56 Howard Street
Belfast
County Antrim
Northern Ireland BT1 6PG
+44 2890248362
www.howardstbelfast.com

Recommended by
Stephen Toman

Opening hours	Closed Monday and Sunday
Credit cards	Accepted
Price range	Affordable
Style	Casual
Cuisine	Mediterranean
Recommended for	Bargain

'Great for pre-theatre.'—Stephen Toman

LITTLE ITALY

13 Amelia Street
Belfast
County Antrim
Northern Ireland BT2 7GS
+44 2890314914

Recommended by
Stephen Toman

Opening hours	Open 7 days
Reservation policy	No
Credit cards	Accepted
Price range	Budget
Style	Casual
Cuisine	Pizza - Takeaway
Recommended for	Late night

'Best pizzas in town.'—Stephen Toman

MOURNE SEAFOOD BAR

Recommended by
Niall McKenna

34–36 Bank Street
Belfast
County Antrim
Northern Ireland BT1 1HL
+44 2890248544
www.mourneseafood.com

Opening hours	Open 7 days
Credit cards	Accepted
Price range	Budget
Style	Casual
Cuisine	Seafood
Recommended for	Bargain

'I tend to pop in here for a pint of prawns or a bowl of mussels. It is a traditional fish restaurant and you get exactly what you ask for.'—Niall McKenna

The flagship branch of Mourne Seafood (there is a another at Dundrum, on the County Down coast) is as pleasantly unpretentious as a seafood restaurant gets. Located in the very heart of the city, down a side alley along from the legendary Belfast pub that is Kelly's Cellars, Mourne's menu always includes hugely generously portions of classic beer-battered fish and chips; a whole grilled catch with boiled buttered potatoes; and oysters and mussels sourced from Mourne's own beds. If you're after something more elaborate – say a seafood risotto or a ceviche – the daily specials have you covered.

THE RAJ

Recommended by
Michael Deane

461 Lisburn Road
Belfast
County Antrim
Northern Ireland BT9 7EQ
+44 2890662168
www.therajbelfast.com

Opening hours	Open 7 days
Credit cards	Accepted
Price range	Affordable
Style	Casual
Cuisine	Indian-Pakistani
Recommended for	Regular neighbourhood

'Great cooking and great friends.'—Michael Deane

SHU

Recommended by
Niall McKenna

253 Lisburn Road
Belfast
County Antrim
Northern Ireland BT9 7EN
+44 2890381655
www.shu-restaurant.com

Opening hours	Closed Sunday
Credit cards	Accepted
Price range	Affordable
Style	Smart casual
Cuisine	British bistro
Recommended for	Regular neighbourhood

'It has classically cooked food and the service and atmosphere are great. It's always a good night out and the chef, Brian McCann, always has something funny to tell you.'—Niall McKenna

THE SPHINX

Recommended by
Michael Deane

74 Stranmillis Road
Belfast
County Antrim
Northern Ireland BT9 5AD
+44 2890681881
www.sphinxkebabs.com

Opening hours	Open 7 days
Reservation policy	No
Credit cards	Not accepted
Price range	Budget
Style	Casual
Cuisine	Kebab Shop
Recommended for	Late night

'Local, fresh and tasty. Owned by famous butcher Earl Jenkins.'—Michael Deane

Laying claim to Belfast's best kebab since 1980, The Sphinx sits in a student-friendly stretch of Stranmillis, in the south of the city. Its doner kebabs have been shortlisted for a national award, the no-nonsense Irish Kebab – just lamb-stuffed pitta without any of that pesky salad – a bestseller. Not that The Sphinx's versatile menu keeps to kebabs, extending to fish 'n' chips, burgers and fried chicken. The exact recipe for their supposedly Egyptian-inspired Sphinx special sauce remains a secret. But it's there on the Sphinx Kebab, Sphinx Burger, Sphinx Fish, Sphinx Chicken Salad and smothered on the Sphinx Chips.

TEDFORDS

Recommended by
Stephen Toman

5 Donegall Quay
Belfast
County Antrim
Northern Ireland BT1 3EA
+44 2890434000
www.tedfordsrestaurant.com

Opening hours	Closed Monday and Sunday
Credit cards	Accepted
Price range	Affordable
Style	Smart casual
Cuisine	Modern French
Recommended for	Local favourite

'One of the longest-serving restaurants in Belfast, showcasing our amazing seafood. Beautiful views overlooking the River Lagan.'—Stephen Toman

RAYANNE HOUSE

Recommended by
Stephen Toman

60 Demense Road
Belfast
County Down
Northern Ireland BT18 9EX
+44 2890425859
www.rayannehouse.com

Opening hours	Open 7 days
Credit cards	Accepted
Price range	Affordable
Style	Casual
Cuisine	British
Recommended for	Breakfast

'Local porridge and yogurt, a great selection for breakfast and child friendly.'—Stephen Toman

BISTRO AT BALLOO HOUSE

Recommended by
Niall McKenna

1 Comber Road
Killinchy
County Down
Northern Ireland BT23 6PA
+44 2897541210
www.ballooinns.com

Opening hours	Open 7 days
Credit cards	Accepted
Price range	Affordable
Style	Casual
Cuisine	British bistro
Recommended for	Local favourite

'I like the fact that the bar always has a turf fire going, no matter what the time of year. The smell always evokes a great sense of familiarity in the big, bustling room. This place is great for Sunday lunch as it is outside of Belfast and supports local producers really well. The menu always has a great selection of fish and meat.'—Niall McKenna

DINING ROOM

Recommended by
Cathal Armstrong

Gregans Castle Hotel
Corkscrew Hill
Ballyvaughan
County Clare
Republic of Ireland
+353 657077005
www.gregans.ie/dining

Opening hours	Closed Wednesday and Sunday
Credit cards	Accepted
Price range	Expensive
Style	Smart casual
Cuisine	Modern Irish
Recommended for	Worth the travel

'It was hands down the best meal I've ever had in Ireland.'—Cathal Armstrong

WILD HONEY INN

Recommended by
Ultan Cooke

Kincora Road
Lisdoonvarna
County Clare
Republic of Ireland
+353 657074300
www.wildhoneyinn.com

Opening hours	Closed Tuesday
Reservation policy	No
Credit cards	Accepted but not AMEX
Price range	Affordable
Style	Casual
Cuisine	Gastropub
Recommended for	Wish I'd opened

'Aidan McGrath is a first-class chef who has a quaint restaurant with a bar and rooms on the west coast. The food is the mature offerings of a chef who has been there, done that and knows what's important.'
—Ultan Cooke

FARMGATE CAFÉ

Recommended by
Ross Lewis

The English Market
Cork
County Cork
Republic of Ireland
+353 214278134
www.farmgate.ie

Opening hours	Closed Sunday
Credit cards	Accepted
Price range	Budget
Style	Casual
Cuisine	Irish
Recommended for	Local favourite

'I think it sums up what is good about Irish food.'
—Ross Lewis

The Cork English Market is even more impressive when viewed from a height, which is just one of the reasons to sit down and tuck into lunch at Kay Harte's daytime Farmgate Café. With an enviably short supply chain, oysters are shucked to order, one of the staff popping downstairs to the fishmonger Pat O'Connell as the need arises. Food is local and the cooking is skilfully simple. Traditional dishes – such as tripe and onions with drisheen (black pudding) and lamb's liver and bacon with champ – can be washed down with craft beer.

HOUSE CAFÉ

Recommended by
Jocky Petrie

Cork Opera House
Emmet Place
Cork
County Cork
Republic of Ireland
+353 214905277

Opening hours	Closed Sunday
Credit cards	Accepted
Price range	Affordable
Style	Casual
Cuisine	Café-Bistro
Recommended for	Bargain

'Best fish I've ever eaten. I've never had a meal here I didn't thoroughly enjoy. Superb desserts too.'
—Jocky Petrie

JACKIE LENNOX CHIP SHOP

Recommended by
Jocky Petrie

137 Bandon Road
Cork
County Cork
Republic of Ireland
+353 214316118

Opening hours	Open 7 days
Reservation policy	No
Credit cards	Not accepted
Price range	Budget
Style	Casual
Cuisine	Fish and Chips
Recommended for	Late night

'There is something unbeatable about their chips. It's the only place I can finish the whole bag every time.'—Jocky Petrie

People in Cork don't go for fish and chips, they go for 'a Lennox's'. Ireland's first purpose-built chippy, opened in 1951 by Jackie and Eileen Lennox on Bandon Road, is still doing its founder proud. From midday until after midnight, the second and third generation Lennoxes turn out the city's best battered cod, haddock and proper chips from the old-fashioned counter. Despite the demand – queues regularly stretch out along the pavement – real attention is paid to produce, so potato, cheese and onion pies are made each morning, chicken and beef are 100 per cent Irish, and cod and haddock fished from sustainable stocks. Even the battered sausage is local.

FISHY FISHY CAFÉ

Recommended by
Paul Flynn,
Ross Lewis

Crowley's Quay
Kinsale
County Cork
Republic of Ireland
+353 214700415
www.fishyfishy.ie

Opening hours	Open 7 days
Credit cards	Accepted but not AMEX
Price range	Affordable
Style	Casual
Cuisine	Seafood
Recommended for	Wish I'd opened

'Always busy because they serve the freshest fish, cooked simply and it is in a beautiful part of Ireland.' —Paul Flynn

Having evolved from a small fish shop that serves a limited number of fish dishes at lunchtime, Martin Shanahan's second, larger Fishy Fishy restaurant has an enviable position at the end of the pier in Kinsale, a fashionable fishing village in Cork. On a sunny day there are few better places to be than the courtyard, in the shade of mature trees, with a bottle of crisp white wine and simply cooked fish from local boats. But it's no secret, so at lunchtime you may have to wait at the bar for a table; they do, however, take bookings for dinner.

BALLYMALOE RESTAURANT

Recommended by
Paul Flynn,
Ross Lewis

Ballymaloe House
Shanagarry
County Cork
Republic of Ireland
+353 214652531
www.ballymaloe.ie

Opening hours	Open 7 days
Credit cards	Accepted
Price range	Expensive
Style	Smart casual
Cuisine	Irish
Recommended for	Breakfast

'They take breakfast very seriously here. Organic porridge and hot breakfasts with free-range bacon and sausages and eggs from the farm.'—Ross Lewis

Not many people know this: you don't need to be staying at Ballymaloe, the renowned country house of the Allen family, to go for breakfast there – a reservation will do. Most of the produce is from their 160-hectare (400-acre) organic farm and just about everything is home-made. Breakfast includes soda bread and scones, and home-made muesli and yogurt, which can be piled up with seasonal fruit such as rhubarb, gooseberries, pears and apples. Eggs are from their own hens, the sausages are from Woodside, the black and white puddings are from Rosscarbery, and there's always fresh fish from nearby Ballycotton.

CHAPTER ONE

Recommended by
Paul Flynn,
Niall McKenna

Basement of Writers Museum
18–19 Parnell Square
Dublin 1
County Dublin
Republic of Ireland
+353 18732266
www.chapteronerestaurant.com

Opening hours	Closed Monday and Sunday
Credit cards	Accepted
Price range	Expensive
Style	Smart casual
Cuisine	Irish
Recommended for	Worth the travel

'True Irish hospitality at its best. You are greeted with a smile and you always feel the welcome. The food is seasonal and local and the service is impeccable.'
—Niall McKenna

Ross Lewis's restaurant beneath the Dublin Writer's Museum is a warm bastion of Irish hospitality at its very best. Housed in the basement of a handsome eighteenth-century townhouse, once the family home of John Jameson of the distilling dynasty, the dining room is a welcoming combination of exposed brickwork and sage-green carpet, its walls hung with work by emerging Irish artists. Lewis's menus champion the very best of Ireland's larder, with a penchant for pork, game and seafood in cooking that's both refined and generous. As befits the building's history, there's a lengthy list of Irish whiskeys for after dinner.

M & L CHINESE RESTAURANT

Recommended by
Ross Lewis

13 Cathedral Street
Dublin 1
County Dublin
Republic of Ireland
+353 18748038
www.mlchineserestaurant.com

Opening hours	Open 7 days
Credit cards	Not accepted
Price range	Affordable
Style	Casual
Cuisine	Szechuan
Recommended for	Late night

'Unexpected' is probably one of the better words to describe this inexpensive Szechuan restaurant, situated down one of Dublin's side streets, which is frequented by the Chinese community and more adventurous diners. For an authentic experience and the full Szechuan heat, either visit with a Chinese friend and order from the Chinese menu, or refuse vehemently to order from the English menu. Pointing to the more interesting dishes being demolished at other tables is one way of doing this, but if there's resistance, insist on 'original' Chinese food, so that the staff choose the dishes and you enjoy the pay-off of your perseverance.

L'ECRIVAIN

Recommended by
Ross Lewis

109a Lower Baggot Street
Dublin 2
County Dublin
Republic of Ireland
+353 16611919
www.lecrivain.com

Opening hours	Closed Sunday
Credit cards	Accepted
Price range	Expensive
Style	Smart casual
Cuisine	French
Recommended for	High end

'It's run by chef Derry Clarke and his wife, Sally Anne, who are building on over twenty-five years of tradition yet still serving first-class food in a warm and friendly environment.'—Ross Lewis

Derry Clarke's established canteen to the Dublin establishment occupies a pair of Georgian coach houses in a courtyard mews off Lower Baggot Street. His sensible response to Ireland's economic ructions was to introduce a three-course lunch menu for a rather reasonable €35 (£29). However, you can still indulge yourself like the Celtic Tiger is ever roaring, as opposed to purring apologetically, with a multi-course tasting menu and a wine list that continues to list magnums of vintage Grands Crus. As always, the cooking showcases the kitchen's fine French technique let loose on the best Irish produce.

THE GREENHOUSE DUBLIN

Recommended by
Ultan Cooke, Paul
Flynn, Jp McMahon

Dawson Street
Dublin 2
County Dublin
Republic of Ireland
+353 16767015
www.thegreenhouserestaurant.ie

Opening hours	Closed Monday and Sunday
Credit cards	Accepted
Price range	Expensive
Style	Smart casual
Cuisine	Modern Irish
Recommended for	High end

'I don't get to Dublin much but The Greenhouse is first class and well worth the trip. It's one to watch – a few more accolades are definitely due.'—Ultan Cooke

RESTAURANT PATRICK GUILBAUD

Recommended by
Paul Flynn

21 Upper Merrion Street
Dublin 2
County Dublin
Republic of Ireland
+353 16764192
www.restaurantpatrickguilbaud.ie

Opening hours	Closed Monday and Sunday
Credit cards	Accepted
Price range	Expensive
Style	Smart casual
Cuisine	Modern French
Recommended for	High end

THE TROCADERO

Recommended by
Kevin Thornton

4 Saint Andrew Street
Dublin 2
County Dublin
Republic of Ireland
+353 16775545
www.trocadero.ie

Opening hours	Open 7 days
Credit cards	Accepted
Price range	Affordable
Style	Smart casual
Cuisine	European
Recommended for	Local favourite

'Late night, great food and staff.'—Kevin Thornton

Long a haunt of Dublin's literati and thespians, the 'Troc' is probably the most nostalgic restaurant in town, filled with old-time showbiz glamour. Liberty-style lampshades, gilt mirrors, bordello-red upholstery and photo-lined walls create a decadent feel, and with the legendary Robert Doggett running the show front of house, the atmosphere is more clubby than restaurant. As the Olympia Theatre is nearby, the pre-theatre menu is popular, but the real action starts later in the evening with people, who all seem to know each other, dropping into the bar or tucking into unpretentious food such as grilled steak and sole on the bone.

VINTAGE COCKTAIL CLUB

Recommended by
Kevin Thornton

15 Crown Alley
Dublin 2
County Dublin
Republic of Ireland
+353 167553547
www.vintagecocktailclub.com

Opening hours	Open 7 days
Credit cards	Accepted
Price range	Affordable
Style	Casual
Cuisine	Irish
Recommended for	Late night

'It's a cool place.'—Kevin Thornton

AVOCA FOOD MARKET & SALT CAFÉ

Recommended by
Kevin Thornton

11a The Crescent
Monkstown
County Dublin
Republic of Ireland
+353 12020230
www.avoca.ie

Opening hours	Open 7 days
Credit cards	Accepted
Price range	Affordable
Style	Casual
Cuisine	Café-Bistro-Deli
Recommended for	Regular neighbourhood

'Family-run restaurant.'—Kevin Thornton

THAT'S AMORE

Recommended by
Ross Lewis

107 Monkstown Road
Monkstown
County Dublin
Republic of Ireland
+353 12845400
www.thatsamoremonkstown.ie

Opening hours	Open 7 days
Credit cards	Accepted
Price range	Affordable
Style	Casual
Cuisine	Italian Bistro
Recommended for	Regular neighbourhood

'Small neighbourhood Italian restaurant run by Marco Valeri and Silvia Leo. Homely atmosphere and they serve good, fresh pasta and pizza.'—Ross Lewis

OWENMORE RESTAURANT

Recommended by
Ultan Cooke

Ballynahinch Castle Hotel
Recess
Connemara
County Galway
Republic of Ireland
+353 9531006
www.ballynahinch-castle.com

Opening hours	Open 7 days
Credit cards	Accepted
Price range	Expensive
Style	Smart casual
Cuisine	Modern Irish
Recommended for	High end

'Set in the unique location of Ballynahinch Castle, it has the whole package with a first-class restaurant. Whenever I can sneak off, this is where I go.'
—Ultan Cooke

ARD BIA AT NIMMOS

Recommended by
Jp McMahon

Spanish Arch
Long Walk
Galway
County Galway
Republic of Ireland
+353 91561114
www.ardbia.com

Opening hours	Open 7 days
Credit cards	Accepted but not AMEX
Price range	Affordable
Style	Casual
Cuisine	Café-Bistro
Recommended for	Breakfast

'Producer-focused menu, wonderful ambience, great location.'—Jp McMahon

ASIAN TEA HOUSE

Recommended by
Ultan Cooke

15 Mary Street
Galway
County Galway
Republic of Ireland
+353 91563749
www.asianteahouse.ie

Opening hours	Closed Tuesday in winter months
Credit cards	Accepted
Price range	Affordable
Style	Casual
Cuisine	Pan-Asian
Recommended for	Late night

'An award-winning Asian restaurant with some real classics that always hit the spot.'—Ultan Cooke

GALWAY FARMERS MARKET

Recommended by
Jp McMahon

Beside St Nicholas's Church
Shop Street
Galway
County Galway
Republic of Ireland
www.galwaymarket.com

Opening hours	Closed Monday to Friday
Reservation policy	No
Credit cards	Not accepted
Price range	Budget
Style	Casual
Cuisine	Street Food
Recommended for	Bargain

'I really enjoy the street food from this market by St Nicholas's Church. There's loads of great food, from falafels to sushi.'—Jp McMahon

KAI CAFÉ & RESTAURANT

Recommended by
Ultan Cooke, Jp McMahon,
Kevin Thornton

20 Sea Road
Galway
County Galway
Republic of Ireland
+353 91526003
www.kaicaferestaurant.com

Opening hours	Open 7 days
Credit cards	Accepted
Price range	Affordable
Style	Casual
Cuisine	Modern Irish
Recommended for	Regular neighbourhood

'Run by Kiwi chef Jess Murphy, Kai is a charming restaurant focusing on local produce and it never fails to wow with real passionate cooking.'—Ultan Cooke

KAPPA-YA

Recommended by
Ultan Cooke

4 Middle Street
Galway
County Galway
Republic of Ireland
+353 91865930
www.kappa-ya.com

Opening hours	Closed Sunday
Credit cards	Accepted but not AMEX
Price range	Affordable
Style	Casual
Cuisine	Japanese
Recommended for	Bargain

'A small Japanese place with some amazing dishes. It's real value for money and, although often quiet, it's where you will find chefs from other restaurants eating lunch on their day off.'—Ultan Cooke

SHERIDANS CHEESEMONGERS

Recommended by
Jp McMahon

14 Church Yard Street
Galway
County Galway
Republic of Ireland
+353 91564832
www.sheridanscheesemongers.com

Opening hours	Closed Monday and Sunday
Reservation policy	No
Credit cards	Accepted but not AMEX
Price range	Affordable
Style	Casual
Cuisine	Bar-Small plates
Recommended for	Late night

'Great wines, fantastic cured Irish meat and artisan raw-milk cheeses from Ireland.'—Jp McMahon

UPSTAIRS@MCCAMBRIDGE'S

Recommended by
Ultan Cooke

McCambridge's of Galway
38–39 Shop Street
Galway
County Galway
Republic of Ireland
+353 91562259
www.mccambridges.com

Opening hours	Open 7 days
Credit cards	Accepted
Price range	Budget
Style	Casual
Cuisine	Café-Bistro-Deli
Recommended for	Breakfast

'An old general store and deli that recently opened a restaurant upstairs, which specalizes in simple hearty fare and seems to get it right on all the little things that count. Their brunch offerings are fantastic.'
—Ultan Cooke

THE HOUSE RESTAURANT

Recommended by
Paul Flynn

Cliff House Hotel
Middle Road
Ardmore
County Waterford
Republic of Ireland
+353 2487800
www.thecliffhousehotel.com

Opening hours	Closed Monday and Sunday
Credit cards	Accepted
Price range	Expensive
Style	Smart casual
Cuisine	Modern Irish
Recommended for	Regular neighbourhood

'One of Ireland's greatest hotel experiences. The food and the view are both spectacular.'—Paul Flynn

GENOA'S TAKEAWAY

Recommended by
Paul Flynn

30 Gratten Square
Dungarvan
County Waterford
Republic of Ireland
+353 5843539

Opening hours	Open 7 days
Reservation policy	No
Credit cards	Not accepted
Price range	Budget
Style	Casual
Cuisine	Fast Food
Recommended for	Late night

'I love their battered sausages.'—Paul Flynn

THE SHAMROCK RESTAURANT

Recommended by
Paul Flynn

4 O'Connell Street
Dungarvan
County Waterford
Republic of Ireland
+353 5842242

Opening hours	Closed Sunday
Credit cards	Accepted but not AMEX
Price range	Budget
Style	Casual
Cuisine	Irish
Recommended for	Breakfast

'Proper, no-nonsense food and always a genuine welcome.'—Paul Flynn

L'ATMOSPHERE

Recommended by
Paul Flynn

19 Henrietta Street
Waterford
County Waterford
Republic of Ireland
+353 51858426
www.restaurant-latmosphere.com

Opening hours	Open 7 days
Credit cards	Accepted but not AMEX
Price range	Affordable
Style	Casual
Cuisine	French Bistro
Recommended for	Bargain

'The best French bistro classics in Ireland.'—Paul Flynn

'THE FOOD IS FILTHY IN ALL THE BEST WAYS.'
NEIL RANKIN P64

'Represents the true side of London'
SAM HARRIS P98

'A FIRST-CLASS FRY UP'
BEN TISH P91

LONDON

'It's almost as though the fish swims from the counter into your mouth – it's that fresh!'
NUNO MENDES P97

'Dangerously addictive and dangerously messy.'
TOM ADAMS P65

'kedgeree and kippers'
SAMI TAMIMI P81

'in-your-face London'
JACOB KENEDY P95

LONDON
WEST

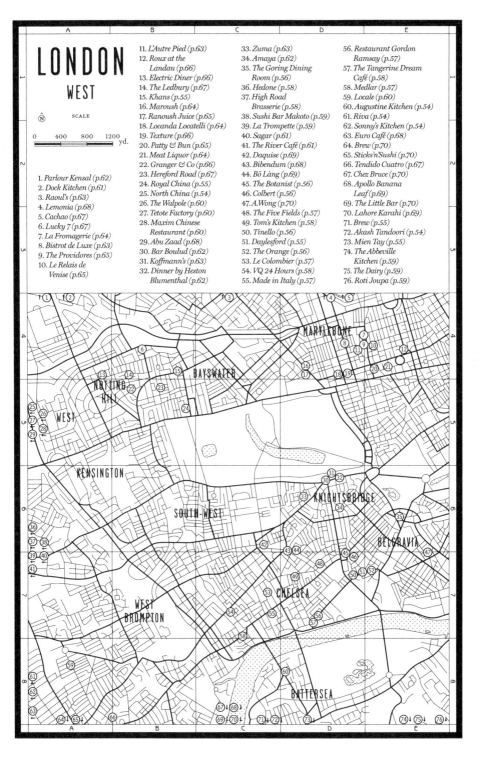

SCALE

0 400 800 1200 yd.

1. *Parlour Kensal (p.62)*
2. *Dock Kitchen (p.61)*
3. *Raoul's (p.63)*
4. *Lemonia (p.68)*
5. *Cachao (p.67)*
6. *Lucky 7 (p.67)*
7. *La Fromagerie (p.64)*
8. *Bistrot de Luxe (p.63)*
9. *The Providores (p.65)*
10. *Le Relais de Venise (p.65)*
11. *L'Autre Pied (p.63)*
12. *Roux at the Landau (p.66)*
13. *Electric Diner (p.66)*
14. *The Ledbury (p.67)*
15. *Khans (p.55)*
16. *Maroush (p.64)*
17. *Ranoush Juice (p.65)*
18. *Locanda Locatelli (p.64)*
19. *Texture (p.66)*
20. *Patty & Bun (p.65)*
21. *Meat Liquor (p.64)*
22. *Granger & Co (p.66)*
23. *Hereford Road (p.67)*
24. *Royal China (p.55)*
25. *North China (p.54)*
26. *The Walpole (p.60)*
27. *Tetote Factory (p.60)*
28. *Maxim Chinese Restaurant (p.60)*
29. *Abu Zaad (p.68)*
30. *Bar Boulud (p.62)*
31. *Koffmann's (p.63)*
32. *Dinner by Heston Blumenthal (p.62)*
33. *Zuma (p.63)*
34. *Amaya (p.62)*
35. *The Goring Dining Room (p.56)*
36. *Hedone (p.58)*
37. *High Road Brasserie (p.58)*
38. *Sushi Bar Makoto (p.59)*
39. *La Trompette (p.59)*
40. *Sagar (p.61)*
41. *The River Café (p.61)*
42. *Daquise (p.69)*
43. *Bibendum (p.68)*
44. *Bō Làng (p.69)*
45. *The Botanist (p.56)*
46. *Colbert (p.56)*
47. *A.Wong (p.70)*
48. *The Five Fields (p.57)*
49. *Tom's Kitchen (p.58)*
50. *Tinello (p.56)*
51. *Daylesford (p.55)*
52. *The Orange (p.56)*
53. *Le Colombier (p.57)*
54. *VQ 24 Hours (p.58)*
55. *Made in Italy (p.57)*
56. *Restaurant Gordon Ramsay (p.57)*
57. *The Tangerine Dream Café (p.58)*
58. *Medlar (p.57)*
59. *Locale (p.60)*
60. *Augustine Kitchen (p.54)*
61. *Riva (p.54)*
62. *Sonny's Kitchen (p.54)*
63. *Euro Café (p.68)*
64. *Brew (p.70)*
65. *Sticks'n'Sushi (p.70)*
66. *Tendido Cuatro (p.67)*
67. *Chez Bruce (p.70)*
68. *Apollo Banana Leaf (p.69)*
69. *The Little Bar (p.70)*
70. *Lahore Karahi (p.69)*
71. *Brew (p.55)*
72. *Akash Tandoori (p.54)*
73. *Mien Tay (p.55)*
74. *The Abbeville Kitchen (p.59)*
75. *The Dairy (p.59)*
76. *Roti Joupa (p.59)*

STREET FEAST
London
+44 7549183866
www.streetfeastlondon.com

Recommended by
Ben Spalding

Opening hours..Variable
Reservation policy...No
Credit cards..Not accepted
Price range...Budget
Style...Casual
Cuisine..Street Food
Recommended for...Late night

'It's a night market and more people need to wake up and see the revolution happening with Street Feast pioneering it!'—Ben Spalding

NORTH CHINA
305 Uxbridge Road
Acton
London W3 9QU
+44 2089929183
www.northchina.co.uk

Recommended by
Henry Harris

Opening hours.......................................Open 7 days
Credit cards...Accepted
Price range..Affordable
Style...Casual
Cuisine...Chinese
Recommended for.....................Regular neighbourhood

'My favourite local. Fresh dumplings and a superb Peking duck served as three or four courses. Family run and damn tasty cooking.'—Henry Harris

RIVA
169 Church Road
Barnes
London SW13 9HR
+44 2087480434

Recommended by
Rainer Becker

Opening hours.......................................Open 7 days
Credit cards...Accepted
Price range..Affordable
Style...Smart casual
Cuisine..Italian
Recommended for.....................Regular neighbourhood

'Riva has great produce. They are so hospitable, but it's low key and the food never lets you down.'
—Rainer Becker

SONNY'S KITCHEN
94 Church Road
Barnes
London SW13 0DQ
+44 2087480393
www.sonnyskitchen.com

Recommended by
Rainer Becker,
Manoj Vasaikar

Opening hours.......................................Open 7 days
Credit cards...Accepted
Price range..Affordable
Style...Smart casual
Cuisine...European
Recommended for.....................Regular neighbourhood

'I think Sonny's is excellent value for money, with menus designed by Phil Howard, a partner in the restaurant.'—Rainer Becker

AKASH TANDOORI
70 Northcote Road
Battersea
London SW11 6QL
+44 8005878129
www.akashtandoori.com

Recommended by
Alyn Williams

Opening hours.......................................Open 7 days
Credit cards...Accepted
Price range...Budget
Style...Casual
Cuisine...Indian
Recommended for...Bargain

'Akash is a Sunday evening family regular. They cook consistently good Indian food that my kids love too.'
—Alyn Williams

AUGUSTINE KITCHEN
63 Battersea Bridge Road
Battersea
London SW11 3AU
+44 2079787085
www.augustine-kitchen.co.uk

Recommended by
Olivier Limousin

Opening hours.......................................Closed Monday
Credit cards...Accepted
Price range..Affordable
Style...Casual
Cuisine..French
Recommended for.....................Regular neighbourhood

'It's very traditional and the chef is very good at classic dishes. I like this restaurant because it looks like a small, French *salle à manger* bistro. Good food and good value for money.'—Olivier Limousin

BREW

Recommended by
Adam Byatt

45 Northcote Road
Battersea
London SW11 1NJ
+44 2075852198
www.brew-cafe.com

Opening hours	Open 7 days
Credit cards	Accepted
Price range	Budget
Style	Casual
Cuisine	Café
Recommended for	Breakfast

'Great coffee. They serve freshly cooked, simple brunch offerings, using impeccable ingredients.'—Adam Byatt

MIEN TAY

Recommended by
Robin Gill

180 Lavender Hill
Battersea
London SW11 5TQ
+44 2073500721
www.mientay.co.uk/battersea

Opening hours	Open 7 days
Credit cards	Not accepted
Price range	Budget
Style	Casual
Cuisine	Vietnamese
Recommended for	Bargain

'The food is exceptional traditional Vietnamese and when you step in you automatically imagine you are in a hectic Saigon restaurant.'—Robin Gill

KHANS

Recommended by
Omar Allibhoy

13–15 Westbourne Grove
Bayswater
London W2 4UA
+44 2077275420
www.khansrestaurant.com

Opening hours	Open 7 days
Credit cards	Accepted
Price range	Budget
Style	Casual
Cuisine	Indian
Recommended for	Wish I'd opened

'It's a place my Indian grandfather used to visit thirty years ago, and it's still kicking ass with the chillies. There is a reason it's been open for so long.'
—Omar Allibhoy

ROYAL CHINA

Recommended by
Margot Henderson, Jacob
Kenedy, Pierre Koffmann,
Thomasina Miers

13 Queensway
Bayswater
London W2 4QJ
+44 2072212535
www.rcguk.co.uk

Opening hours	Open 7 days
Credit cards	Accepted
Price range	Affordable
Style	Casual
Cuisine	Chinese
Recommended for	Bargain

'I love dim sum for breakfast more than anything.'
—Jacob Kenedy

DAYLESFORD

Recommended by
Tom Aikens

44b Pimlico Road
Belgravia
London SW1W 8LP
+44 2078818060
www.daylesford.com

Opening hours	Open 7 days
Reservation policy	No
Credit cards	Accepted
Price range	Affordable
Style	Casual
Cuisine	British bistro
Recommended for	Breakfast

'Fantastic seasonal fare, farm fresh and organic!'
—Tom Aikens

THE GORING DINING ROOM

Recommended by
Chris Galvin

The Goring
15 Beeston Place
Belgravia
London SW1W 0JW
+44 2073969000
www.thegoring.com

Opening hours	Open 7 days
Credit cards	Accepted
Price range	Expensive
Style	Smart casual
Cuisine	British
Recommended for	High end

'When celebrating a special family occasion, we combine a visit to the restaurant with a stay at this amazing hotel.'—Chris Galvin

Owned and run by the Goring family for over a century, this luxury Belgravia hotel was appointed a Royal Warrant on its 100th anniversary in 2010. From serving as a plush command centre for the Chief of Allied Forces during World War I, to being the bride's family base for the Royal Wedding in 2011, it has always served the establishment. Its dining room, revamped in 2005 by Viscount Linley, remains a bastion of Britishness, where lunch is still called 'luncheon' and the trolley is laden with roast lamb, steak and kidney pie or roast beef. If class and grace are boring, then The Goring is a snorefest.

THE ORANGE

Recommended by
Tom Aikens

37 Pimlico Road
Belgravia
London SW1W 8NE
+44 2078819844
www.theorange.co.uk

Opening hours	Open 7 days
Credit cards	Accepted
Price range	Affordable
Style	Casual
Cuisine	British bistro
Recommended for	Breakfast

'Has a great kids menu, perfect for my young daughter.'
—Tom Aikens

TINELLO

Recommended by
Giorgio Locatelli

87 Pimlico Road
Belgravia
London SW1W 8PH
+44 2077303663
www.tinello.co.uk

Opening hours	Closed Sunday
Credit cards	Accepted but not Diners
Price range	Affordable
Style	Smart casual
Cuisine	Tuscan
Recommended for	Regular neighbourhood

'Friendly and relaxed atmosphere, and Tuscan food in welcoming surroundings.'—Giorgio Locatelli

THE BOTANIST

Recommended by
Heinz Beck

7 Sloane Square
Chelsea
London SW1W 8EE
+44 2077300077
www.thebotanistonsloanesquare.com

Opening hours	Open 7 days
Credit cards	Accepted
Price range	Affordable
Style	Casual
Cuisine	European
Recommended for	Breakfast

'When I am in London, I breakfast at the Botanist as I prefer to start my day lightly with a glass of their freshly squeezed orange juice and a plate of fresh fruit, usually mango and papaya.'—Heinz Beck

COLBERT

Recommended by
Tom Aikens,
Pascal Aussignac,
Marcus Wareing

50–52 Sloane Square
Chelsea
London SW1W 8AX
+44 2077302804
www.colbertchelsea.com

Opening hours	Open 7 days
Credit cards	Accepted
Price range	Affordable
Style	Casual
Cuisine	French Brasserie
Recommended for	Breakfast

'It's great for meetings but equally I can go with my son for a bacon sandwich and cup of tea and fit right in.'
—Marcus Wareing

LE COLOMBIER

Recommended by
Pierre Koffmann

145 Dovehouse Street
Chelsea
London SW3 6LB
+44 2073511155
www.le-colombier-restaurant.co.uk

Opening hours	Open 7 days
Credit cards	Accepted
Price range	Affordable
Style	Casual
Cuisine	French
Recommended for	Regular neighbourhood

'Proper classic French food and friendly service. I go for the *plateaux de fruits de mer* (seafood platters) and *chaud froid aux amandes* (ice cream with chocolate sauce and almonds).'—Pierre Koffmann

THE FIVE FIELDS

Recommended by
Pierre Koffmann

8–9 Blacklands Terrace
Chelsea
London SW3 2SP
+44 2078381082
www.fivefieldsrestaurant.com

Opening hours	Closed Monday and Sunday
Credit cards	Accepted
Price range	Expensive
Style	Smart casual
Cuisine	Modern British
Recommended for	High end

'Proper fine dining.'—Pierre Koffmann

MADE IN ITALY

Recommended by
Alyn Williams

249 Kings Road
Chelsea
London SW3 5EL
+44 2073521880
www.madeinitalygroup.co.uk

Opening hours	Open 7 days
Credit cards	Accepted
Price range	Budget
Style	Casual
Cuisine	Italian
Recommended for	Regular neighbourhood

'They serve simple, delicious, wood-fired pizzas with friendly service.'—Alyn Williams

MEDLAR

Recommended by
Mikael Jonsson,
Neil Rankin,
Marcus Wareing

438 Kings Road
Chelsea
London SW10 0LJ
+44 2073491900
www.medlarrestaurant.co.uk

Opening hours	Open 7 days
Credit cards	Accepted
Price range	Affordable
Style	Casual
Cuisine	Modern European
Recommended for	Regular neighbourhood

'It's actually not that pricey, but going there always makes an occasion. Its perfectly pitched service makes you feel special but also puts you at ease. The wine selection and cheese trolley are worthy of a trip all by themselves but it's the attention to detail in its Frenchified nod to the classics menu that wins me over. There are no foams, jellies or spheres here, it's just a menu you enjoy reading almost as much as eating.'—Neil Rankin

RESTAURANT GORDON RAMSAY

Recommended by
Paul Owens,
Ben Spalding

68 Royal Hospital Road
Chelsea
London SW3 4HP
+44 2073524441
www.gordonramsay.com/royalhospitalroad

Opening hours	Closed Saturday and Sunday
Credit cards	Accepted
Price range	Expensive
Style	Formal
Cuisine	European
Recommended for	High end

'The benchmark in London. A restaurant and kitchen that taught me many disciplines when I trained there.'—Ben Spalding

THE TANGERINE DREAM CAFÉ

Recommended by
Theo Randall

Chelsea Physic Garden
66 Royal Hospital Road
Chelsea
London SW3 4HS
+44 2073496464
www.tangerinedream.uk.com

Opening hours	Closed Monday and Saturday
Reservation policy	No
Credit cards	Accepted
Price range	Affordable
Style	Casual
Cuisine	Café
Recommended for	Local favourite

'One of my favourite local places. In the summer months, Limpet Barron opens her café in the evenings and cooks delicious food in the oldest and most beautiful garden in Central London.'—Theo Randall

TOM'S KITCHEN

Recommended by
Clare Smyth

27 Cale Street
Chelsea
London SW3 3QP
+44 2073490202
www.tomskitchen.co.uk

Opening hours	Open 7 days
Credit cards	Accepted
Price range	Affordable
Style	Casual
Cuisine	British bistro
Recommended for	Breakfast

VQ 24 HOURS

Recommended by
Steffen Hansen

325 Fulham Road
Chelsea
London SW10 9QL
+44 2073767224
www.vq24hours.com

Opening hours	Open 7 days
Credit cards	Accepted
Price range	Budget
Style	Casual
Cuisine	International
Recommended for	Late night

'The name says it all, open 24/7. Where else can you drink a bottle of Krug in the early-morning hours?' —Steffen Hansen

HEDONE

Recommended by
Daniel Berlin,
Stephen Harris

301–303 Chiswick High Road
Chiswick
London W4 4HH
+44 2087470377
www.hedonerestaurant.com

Opening hours	Closed Monday and Sunday
Credit cards	Accepted
Price range	Expensive
Style	Smart casual
Cuisine	Modern European
Recommended for	Worth the travel

'It's only about the produce!'—Daniel Berlin

Mikael Jonsson has come a long way: severe food allergies meant he first became a lawyer and then an ingredient-obsessed blogger. When he finally opened this Chiswick restaurant in 2011 it secured a Michelin star in just fourteen months. Its name roughly translates as 'pleasure', and the same earnestness dictates the room's look, with bare bricks and a very open-plan kitchen. There's no fixed menu, but instead a long and elegant procession of dishes celebrating the very best British ingredients such as wild Dorset turbot and Cornish rock oysters. A recent nod from San Pellegrino should see more customers schlepping to the 'burbs.

HIGH ROAD BRASSERIE

Recommended by
Manoj Vasaikar

162–170 Chiswick High Road
Chiswick
London W4 1PR
+44 2087427474
www.brasserie.highroadhouse.co.uk

Opening hours	Open 7 days
Credit cards	Accepted
Price range	Affordable
Style	Casual
Cuisine	European
Recommended for	Breakfast

'Very casual, nice atmosphere. Lean breakfast.' —Manoj Vasaikar

SUSHI BAR MAKOTO

Recommended by
Sami Tamimi

57 Turnham Green Terrace
Chiswick
London W4 1RP
+44 2089873180
www.sushibarmakato.co.uk

Opening hours	Closed Monday
Credit cards	Accepted
Price range	Affordable
Style	Casual
Cuisine	Sushi
Recommended for	Local favourite

'The thing I love most about London is that you can be transported all over the world through kitchens within a few square miles. Makoto is just one of these: the sushi you are served is second to none. The welcome that customers get from the couple who run the bar is so warm that you feel as though you've been invited to their house.'—Sami Tamimi

LA TROMPETTE

Recommended by
Manoj Vasaikar

3–7 Devonshire Road
Chiswick
London W4 2EU
+44 2087471836
www.latrompette.co.uk

Opening hours	Open 7 days
Credit cards	Accepted
Price range	Affordable
Style	Smart casual
Cuisine	Modern European
Recommended for	Regular neighbourhood

THE ABBEVILLE KITCHEN

Recommended by
Jonathan Jones

47 Abbeville Road
Clapham
London SW4 9JX
+44 2087721110
www.abbevillekitchen.com

Opening hours	Open 7 days
Credit cards	Accepted
Price range	Affordable
Style	Casual
Cuisine	European
Recommended for	Breakfast

'They have the best bacon and sausages from George at Swaledale. Great for lunch and dinner too.'
—Jonathan Jones

THE DAIRY

Recommended by
Tom Aikens

15 The Pavement
Clapham
London SW4 0HY
+44 2076224165
www.the-dairy.co.uk

Opening hours	Closed Monday
Credit cards	Accepted
Price range	Affordable
Style	Casual
Cuisine	British bistro
Recommended for	Bargain

'A lovely local with a good vibe. Good-quality ingredients, partly sourced from their own garden, and a good level of cooking with a British seasonal approach.'—Tom Aikens

ROTI JOUPA

Recommended by
Jonathan Jones

12 Clapham High Street
Clapham
London SW4 7UT
+44 2076278637
www.rotijoupa.com

Opening hours	Closed Sunday
Reservation policy	No
Credit cards	Not accepted
Price range	Budget
Style	Casual
Cuisine	Caribbean
Recommended for	Late night

'Impeccable *roti* (unleavened bread) and curried goat. The freshest take away food I know.'
—Jonathan Jones

MAXIM CHINESE RESTAURANT
Recommended by
Alfred Prasad

153–155 Northfield Avenue
Ealing
London W13 9QT
+44 2085671719
www.maxim-ealing.co.uk

Opening hours	Open 7 days
Credit cards	Accepted
Price range	Affordable
Style	Casual
Cuisine	Chinese
Recommended for	Regular neighbourhood

'Everybody should have a neighbourhood gem they feel proud of. Maxim is largely family run and the service is friendly and relaxed, which really hits the right note for a neighbourhood restaurant. It has a lovely, warm and elegant ambience, filled with regular patrons every day of the week. The highlight of Maxim is its freshly made, tasty food. Many times I've seen the big boss herself, Mrs Chow, supervising the kitchen. Her high standards are clearly reflected in the delicious and consistent dishes. My favourites there are prawns in ginger and spring onions and the plain noodles. And I highly recommend the salt-and-pepper squid, salt-and-pepper fine beans and the barbeque pork ribs which are delicately spiced and beautifully cooked.'—Alfred Prasad

TETOTE FACTORY
Recommended by
Jocky Petrie

12 South Ealing Road
Ealing
London W5 4QA
+44 2085798391
www.tetotefactory.co.uk

Opening hours	Closed Monday
Reservation policy	No
Credit cards	Accepted but not AMEX
Price range	Budget
Style	Casual
Cuisine	Bakery
Recommended for	Breakfast

'I'm not a big breakfast person, but this tiny bakery is great. Their bread is made with a Japanese twist. The chocolate brioche is very good, as are their baguettes.'
—Jocky Petrie

THE WALPOLE
Recommended by
Jocky Petrie

35 St Mary's Road
Ealing
London W5 5RG
+44 2085677918
www.walpole-ealing.co.uk

Opening hours	Closed Monday and Sunday
Credit cards	Accepted but not AMEX
Price range	Affordable
Style	Casual
Cuisine	European Bistro
Recommended for	Bargain

'The portions are huge and the food delicious. There's a great atmosphere too.'—Jocky Petrie

LOCALE
Recommended by
Omar Allibhoy

222 Munster Road
Fulham
London SW6 6AY
+44 2073816137
www.localerestaurants.com

Opening hours	Open 7 days
Credit cards	Accepted
Price range	Affordable
Style	Casual
Cuisine	Italian
Recommended for	Late night

'I always end up at this great Italian restaurant which serves a proper seafood linguine. Whenever I order that dish it never disappoints!'—Omar Allibhoy

THE RIVER CAFÉ

Thames Wharf
Rainville Road
Hammersmith
London W6 9HA
+44 2073864200
www.rivercafe.co.uk

Recommended by
Rainer Becker, Samantha &
Samuel Clark, Andreas Dahlberg
Jeff Galvin, Alexis Gauthier,
Gabrielle Hamilton, Philip
Howard, Jeremy Lee, James
Lowe, Niall McKenna, Thomasina
Miers, Rafael Osterling, Stevie
Parle, Tim Siadatan, Roberta
Sudbrack, Sami Tamimi, Peter
Weeden, Junya Yamasaki

Opening hours	Open 7 days
Credit cards	Accepted
Price range	Expensive
Style	Smart casual
Cuisine	Italian
Recommended for	High end

'A brilliant story of two women opening a restaurant. They were at an age when many are thinking of retiring. It is pioneering stuff. It thrives and has spurred on so many cooks. A lunch on its lovely terrace in the sunshine remains one of life's great pleasures.' —Jeremy Lee

Italian food made by Ruth Rogers and her team with the very best produce money can buy, assembled in neo-rustic style, served in a stylish modern glass-fronted canteen (originally an old oil storage facility before architect Richard Rogers got hold of it), down where the old Thames does flow. That's been the River Café's formula for success since it opened in 1988. Co-founder Rose Gray, who sadly passed away in 2010, would be pleased to see nothing has changed in her absence. Perfect setting meets perfect produce, meets educated service and a wine list, aside from the odd Champagne, that is all-Italian and runs from humble bottles to Super Tuscans.

SAGAR

157 King Street
Hammersmith
London W6 9JT
+44 2087418563
www.sagarveg.co.uk

Recommended by
Martin Morales

Opening hours	Open 7 days
Credit cards	Accepted
Price range	Budget
Style	Casual
Cuisine	Indian-Vegetarian
Recommended for	Bargain

'Freshly made Indian vegetarian food with tasty ingredients, like a masala dosa and a lunch for £6 which includes some eight items.' —Martin Morales

DOCK KITCHEN

Portobello Docks
342–344 Ladbroke Grove
Kensal Green
London W10 5BU
+44 2089621610
www.dockkitchen.co.uk

Recommended by
Samantha & Samuel Clark,
Thomasina Miers

Opening hours	Open 7 days
Credit cards	Accepted
Price range	Affordable
Style	Smart casual
Cuisine	International
Recommended for	Regular neighbourhood

'Stevie is a very talented chef and as he, like us, trained at the River Café, his approach and food combinations feel very natural to us. The restaurant is also part of Tom Dixon's unique studio near Ladbroke Grove, which in itself is very striking and beautiful.' —Samantha & Samuel Clark

PARLOUR KENSAL

5 Regent Street
Kensal Green
London NW10 5LG
+44 2089692184
www.parlourkensal.com

Recommended by
James Knappett

Opening hours	Closed Monday
Credit cards	Accepted
Price range	Affordable
Style	Casual
Cuisine	Gastropub
Recommended for	Regular neighbourhood

'It's a proper British pub, but the chef really brings the food alive and really makes it interesting, with some great ingredients. There are nice touches, like how you can make your own toast.'—James Knappett

AMAYA

Halkin Arcade
Motcomb Street
Knightsbridge
London SW1X 8JT
+44 2078231166
www.amaya.biz

Recommended by
Manoj Vasaikar

Opening hours	Open 7 days
Credit cards	Accepted
Price range	Expensive
Style	Smart casual
Cuisine	Modern Indian
Recommended for	Wish I'd opened

'Most chic Indian grill in town and a great atmosphere.'
—Manoj Vasaikar

BAR BOULUD

Mandarin Oriental Hyde Park
66 Knightsbridge
Knightsbridge
London SW1X 7LA
+44 2072013899
www.barboulud.com

Recommended by
Paul Foster, Francesco
Mazzei, Glynn Purnell, Clare
Smyth, Marcus Wareing

Opening hours	Open 7 days
Credit cards	Accepted
Price range	Affordable
Style	Smart casual
Cuisine	French
Recommended for	Late night

'The food is simple and approachable, but is of an amazing standard. The service is relaxed and friendly with the attention to detail of a thirty-seat Michelin-starred restaurant.'—Paul Foster

A restaurant in a five-star hotel in the heart of Knightsbridge might seem an unlikely late-night hang-out for anyone other than the supremely wealthy and unimaginative, but then Bar Boulud isn't your typical operation. Firstly, the French bistro-style food, with all manner of charcuterie and tempting titbits, is much more accessible than many hotels offer. Secondly, it does a seriously good burger, including the traditional-style Yankee, the Frenchie (made with confit pork belly and Morbier) and the Piggie (BBQ pulled pork and green chilli mayonnaise). What's more, you can wash it down with one of their uncommonly large selection of draught beers.

DINNER BY HESTON BLUMENTHAL

Mandarin Oriental Hyde Park
66 Knightsbridge
Knightsbridge
London SW1X 7LA
+44 2072013833
www.dinnerbyheston.com

Recommended by
Omar Allibhoy,
Tomi Björck, Christian
Domschitz, Brian Mark
Hansen, Timothy Johnson,
Tony Mantuano, Shuko Oda,
Tom Sellers, Jock Zonfrillo

Opening hours	Open 7 days
Credit cards	Accepted
Price range	Expensive
Style	Smart casual
Cuisine	Modern British
Recommended for	Worth the travel

'As my English husband said as we left Dinner one time, "I'm proud to be English". That's how good the meal was. I did not know pork chops could taste that good. The best ingredients cooked to perfection. I'm not usually one for sweets, but dessert was astonishing.'
—Shuko Oda

Heston Blumenthal's Fat Duck follow-up is a bustling brasserie with a playful menu, much of it surprisingly straightforward despite being inspired by a geeky love of British food history. Overlooking Hyde Park from the handsome rear of Knightsbridge's Mandarin Oriental, its spacious dining room seats 136 at large, luxuriously spaced tables. Inside the vast glass-fronted kitchen, a giant Swiss watch movement turning a series of spits catches the eye. So too the now trademark Meat Fruit – a chicken liver parfait made to resemble a mandarin – and the Tipsy Cake – vanilla-custard-filled brioche served with pineapple roasted on that showcase rotisserie.

KOFFMANN'S

Recommended by
Jacob Kenedy, Tom Kitchin

The Berkeley
Wilton Place
Knightsbridge
London SW1X 7RL
+44 2071078844
www.the-berkeley.co.uk/koffmanns

Opening hours	Open 7 days
Credit cards	Accepted
Price range	Affordable
Style	Smart casual
Cuisine	French
Recommended for	Regular neighbourhood

'I worked with Pierre Koffmann for five years and
I always try to go to The Berkeley when I'm in London.
Even after all these years he's still my mentor and
I really enjoy spending time with him. For me, Chef
is a genius and I love his cooking.'—Tom Kitchin

ZUMA

Recommended by
Heinz Beck, Thomas Bühner,
Andreas Caminada, Gert de
Mangeleer, Henry Harris,
Matthew Harris, Alfonso &
Ernesto Iaccarino, Francesco
Mazzei, Theo Randall, Shaun
Rankin, Agnar Sverrisson,
Mitch Tonks, Ricardo Zarate

5 Raphael Street
Knightsbridge
London SW7 1DL
+44 2075841010
www.zumarestaurant.com

Opening hours	Open 7 days
Credit cards	Accepted
Price range	Expensive
Style	Smart casual
Cuisine	Japanese
Recommended for	Wish I'd opened

'Zuma has a fabulous atmosphere coupled with great
food and hospitality. They excel on freshness and the
quality of their product and you'd be hard pushed to
find better Japanese food in London. I can highly
recommend the salt-grilled sea bass and the wagyu
beef.'—Shaun Rankin

RAOUL'S

Recommended by
Pierre Koffman

13 Clifton Road
Maida Vale
London W9 1SZ
+44 2072897313
www.raoulsgourmet.com

Opening hours	Open 7 days
Credit cards	Accepted
Price range	Affordable
Style	Casual
Cuisine	European Bistro
Recommended for	Breakfast

L'AUTRE PIED

Recommended by
Ben Spalding

5–7 Blandford Street
Marylebone
London W1U 3DB
+44 2074869696
www.lautrepied.co.uk

Opening hours	Open 7 days
Credit cards	Accepted
Price range	Expensive
Style	Smart casual
Cuisine	Modern French
Recommended for	Local favourite

'An accessible, brilliant, everyday restaurant that is
there for the customer, not for ego. Good value and it
has a brilliantly talented chef in Andy McFadden. Just
a well-rounded restaurant.'—Ben Spalding

BISTROT DE LUXE

Recommended by
Omar Allibhoy, Paul Flynn,
Martin Morales

66 Baker Street
Marylebone
London W1U 7DJ
+44 2079354007
www.galvinrestaurants.com

Opening hours	Open 7 days
Credit cards	Accepted
Price range	Affordable
Style	Smart casual
Cuisine	French
Recommended for	Regular neighbourhood

'A perfectly French, buzzy bistro, with wonderfully rich
and perfectly executed food.'—Paul Flynn

LA FROMAGERIE

Recommended by
Omar Allibhoy

2–6 Moxon Street
Marylebone
London W1U 4EW
+44 2079350341
www.lafromagerie.co.uk

Opening hours	Open 7 days
Reservation policy	No
Credit cards	Accepted
Price range	Affordable
Style	Casual
Cuisine	Deli-Café
Recommended for	Breakfast

'This is, in my opinion, the best place to buy cheese in London. You can also purchase quality, fresh produce here. The breakfast is fantastic and the best ingredients are always used. However, be warned, it's not cheap.'
—Omar Allibhoy

LOCANDA LOCATELLI

Recommended by
Yotam Ottolenghi

8 Seymour Street
Marylebone
London W1H 7JZ
+44 2079359088
www.locandalocatelli.com

Opening hours	Open 7 days
Credit cards	Accepted but not Diners
Price range	Expensive
Style	Smart casual
Cuisine	Modern Italian
Recommended for	High end

'It's the most solid of all of London's Italian restaurants. You know exactly what you are going to get, in the best possible sense: delicious, comfortable luxury. For pure comfort, I'd always have the home-made dumplings with cep mushrooms.'—Yotam Ottolenghi

MAROUSH

Recommended by
Sat Bains, Ruth Rogers

21 Edgware Road
Marylebone
London W2 2JE
+44 2077230773
www.maroush.com

Opening hours	Open 7 days
Credit cards	Accepted
Price range	Affordable
Style	Smart casual
Cuisine	Lebanese
Recommended for	Late night

MEAT LIQUOR

Recommended by
Adam Byatt, Michael Deane,
André Garrett, Tom Kerridge,
Neil Rankin, Tom Sellers,
Karam Sethi

74 Welbeck Street
Marylebone
London W1G 0BA
www.meatliquor.com

Opening hours	Open 7 days
Reservation policy	No
Credit cards	Accepted
Price range	Budget
Style	Casual
Cuisine	Burgers
Recommended for	Late night

'Meat Liquor is as far from fine dining as dining out gets. It's dark, loud and busy and the food is filthy in all the best ways. It's the antithesis of almost everything chefs and restaurateurs try to achieve and this is possibly the reason so many of them come here. The food isn't perfect but nothing fills a hole better than a Dead Hippie burger and some chilli cheese fries, especially after a few ales. This is a burger joint that leaves all the others here and in the States for dust and wishing they'd thought of it first.'—Neil Rankin

Meat Liquor – born in late 2011, the child of the rather rock 'n' roll burger van turned pop-up – produces burgers, Philly cheese steaks, chilli dogs, buffalo wings, peanut butter sundaes and so on – all of which, unlike many others, aren't a sad, pale imitation of what you find stateside. The bar does a good selection of microbrews and no-nonsense cocktails served in jars that don't skimp on the liquor. That the queues of trendy young tattooed things waiting to sink their teeth into a Dead Hippy haven't shortened, even since they opened several additional outposts (Meat Market in Covent Garden; Meat Mission in Shoreditch; another Meat Liquor in Brighton), is testament to their success.

PATTY & BUN

Recommended by
Tom Adams, Karam Sethi

54 James Street
Marylebone
London W1U 1HE
+44 2074873188
www.pattyandbun.co.uk

Opening hours	Closed Monday
Reservation policy	No
Credit cards	Accepted
Price range	Budget
Style	Casual
Cuisine	Burgers
Recommended for	Bargain

'For me, they produce the best burgers in town. Dangerously addictive and dangerously messy. I averaged three a week at one point, which is always a worry.'—Tom Adams

THE PROVIDORES AND TAPA ROOM

Recommended by
Brad Farmerie

109 Marylebone High Street
Marylebone
London W1U 4RX
+44 2079356175
www.theprovidores.co.uk

Opening hours	Open 7 days
Credit cards	Accepted
Price range	Affordable
Style	Casual
Cuisine	Modern International
Recommended for	Breakfast

'Amazing, big punches of flavour, super attentive service, in a relaxed atmosphere – what brunch is all about.'—Brad Farmerie

This Marylebone High Street establishment has been the darling of London brunchers since 2001. Come any time of day and you'll be welcomed by smiling service and knockout blends of flavour, but breakfasts in the Tapa Room will exceed your wildest dreams. Chef Peter Gordon creates true fusion food without forgetting his Kiwi roots, which is reflected in the wine list that includes Bellinis made with New Zealand sparkling wine. Popular favourites include Turkish (poached) eggs with whipped yogurt and hot chilli butter on sourdough, or grilled chorizo with sweet potato and miso mash, garlic labneh and star anise cashew nut praline. A solid Bloody Mary, tamarillo and kiwi fruit smoothies, and excellent coffee provide a memorable morning hit.

RANOUSH JUICE

Recommended by
Henry Harris,
Steve Williams

43 Edgware Road
Marylebone
London W2 2JE
+44 2077235929
www.maroush.com

Opening hours	Open 7 days
Reservation policy	No
Credit cards	Not accepted
Price range	Budget
Style	Casual
Cuisine	Lebanese
Recommended for	Late night

'Open late into the night serving some of the best shawarmas in London. A lamb shawarma kebab and a fresh melon juice will help abate an impending hangover.'—Steve Williams

Even East Enders on a 3.00 a.m. kebab hunt have been known to end up at this Edgware Road staple from the Maroush empire, long overlords of so-called Little Beirut. It's a little rough and ready – there are seats for twenty, but most treat it as a take away, and boozy queues inevitably gather in the small hours – but benefits from an expert Lebanese production line. The shawarma kebabs are first-rate, whether carved onto the plate or slathered with hummus and pickles in a sandwich, while mezze, baklava and fresh fruit juices offer further fortification for those braving an all-nighter.

LE RELAIS DE VENISE

Recommended by
Ollie Dabbous

120 Marylebone Lane
Marylebone
London W1U 2QG
+44 2074860878
www.relaisdevenise.com

Opening hours	Open 7 days
Reservation policy	No
Credit cards	Accepted
Price range	Affordable
Style	Casual
Cuisine	French
Recommended for	Regular neighbourhood

ROUX AT THE LANDAU

Recommended by
Jacob Kenedy

The Langham
1c Portland Place
Marylebone
London W1B 1JA
+44 2079650165
www.thelandau.com

Opening hours	Open 7 days
Credit cards	Accepted
Price range	Expensive
Style	Smart casual
Cuisine	Modern French
Recommended for	High end

'Chris in the kitchen and Franco on the floor are at the top of their games. Cocktails in the adjoining artisan bar are enough to knock anyone for six.'
—Jacob Kenedy

TEXTURE

Recommended by
Raymond Blanc

34 Portman Street
Marylebone
London W1H 7BY
+44 2072240028
www.texture-restaurant.co.uk

Opening hours	Closed Monday and Sunday
Credit cards	Accepted
Price range	Expensive
Style	Smart casual
Cuisine	Modern European
Recommended for	Regular neighbourhood

'My favourite restaurant at the moment is Texture – it's absolutely wonderful. A wonderful menu and stunning wine list – what more could you ask for?'
—Raymond Blanc

Agnar Sverrisson and Xavier Rousset absconded from Raymond Blanc's famed Oxford restaurant Le Manoir aux Quat'Saisons, where they were head chef and head sommelier, to open their smart Champagne bar and restaurant in the capital. The menu is modern European, but Sverrisson's Icelandic background brings additional Scandinavian flair to the proceedings, while Rousset pulls out all the stops with a wine list of more than 100 different bottles of bubbly alone. To experience it at its best, ditch the à la carte and opt for the Scandinavian fish-tasting menu. Order a bottle of Pol Roger Sir Winston Churchill '99 to wash down the Icelandic cod.

ELECTRIC DINER

Recommended by
Karam Sethi

191 Portobello Road
Notting Hill
London W11 2ED
+44 2079089696
www.electricdiner.com

Opening hours	Open 7 days
Credit cards	Accepted
Price range	Affordable
Style	Casual
Cuisine	Diner-Café
Recommended for	Wish I'd opened

'I like the menu and brasserie style of the restaurant, especially since its reopening. It's also a great concept to have the cinema right next door, especially in a neighbourhood like Notting Hill. Not only is it packed for dinner but weekend brunch is always full.'
—Karam Sethi

GRANGER & CO

Recommended by
Tom Aikens

175 Westbourne Grove
Notting Hill
London W11 2SB
+44 2072299111
www.grangerandco.com

Opening hours	Open 7 days
Reservation policy	No
Credit cards	Accepted
Price range	Affordable
Style	Casual
Cuisine	Modern Australian
Recommended for	Breakfast

'Healthy and light breakfast and brunch options in a nice, relaxing environment.'—Tom Aikens

HEREFORD ROAD

3 Hereford Road
Notting Hill
London W2 4AB
+44 2077271144
www.herefordroad.org

Recommended by
Ollie Dabbous, Marcus
Eaves, Thomasina Miers

Opening hours	Open 7 days
Credit cards	Accepted
Price range	Affordable
Style	Casual
Cuisine	British
Recommended for	Regular neighbourhood

'Hereford Road is my favourite neighbourhood
restaurant. It showcases simple, hearty British cooking.
Hereford Road is simple, honest cooking at its best.'
—Marcus Eaves

The West London chapter of the school of St. John,
Hereford Road first brought its gutsy, no-nonsense
cooking built around British seasonal ingredients to
nearby Notting Hill in 2007. Driven by hardworking
chef-proprietor Tom Pemberton, formerly head chef
of St. John Bread & Wine, it's housed in a Victorian
butcher's shop, open kitchen in the window where
the counter would have been, wrought ironwork
on the ceiling above the red leather upholstered
loveseats. The daily-changing menu delivers perfect
simplicity, from whole fish and helpings of offal to
bowls of rice pudding and jam. Their set lunch
remains one of London's great bargains.

THE LEDBURY

127 Ledbury Road
Notting Hill
London W11 2AQ
+44 2077929090
www.theledbury.com

Recommended by
Jason Atherton, Galton
Blackiston, Samantha &
Samuel Clark, Matthew
Gaudet, Esben Holmboe
Bang, Mikael Jonsson,
Scot Kirton, Isaac McHale,
Thomasina Miers, Jocky
Petrie, Ben Spalding, Adam
Stokes, Steve Williams

Opening hours	Open 7 days
Credit cards	Accepted
Price range	Expensive
Style	Smart casual
Cuisine	Modern European
Recommended for	High end

'Still the best fine dining in the UK.'—Isaac McHale

LUCKY 7

127 Westbourne Park Road
Notting Hill
London W2 5QL
+44 2077276771
www.lucky7london.co.uk

Recommended by
Thomasina Miers

Opening hours	Open 7 days
Reservation policy	No
Credit cards	Accepted but not AMEX or Diners
Price range	Budget
Style	Casual
Cuisine	Diner
Recommended for	Bargain

TENDIDO CUATRO

108–110 New Kings Road
Parsons Green
London SW6 4LY
+44 2073715147
www.cambiodetercio.co.uk

Recommended by
Alexis Gauthier

Opening hours	Open 7 days
Credit cards	Accepted
Price range	Affordable
Style	Casual
Cuisine	Spanish
Recommended for	Regular neighbourhood

'I go almost every Sunday with my family. For me,
this epitomises what a restaurant should be like:
simply somewhere you want to go to, with the people
you love, over and over again. The food is good, lots
of interesting flavours at a steady pace, which only
the Spanish can do. But it is the service and the
atmosphere they really get right. You can tell they
love their customers.'—Alexis Gauthier

CACHAO

140 Regents Park Road
Primrose Hill
London NW1 8XL
+44 2074834422
www.cachaotoycafe.com

Recommended by
Theo Randall

Opening hours	Open 7 days
Credit cards	Accepted
Price range	Budget
Style	Casual
Cuisine	Café
Recommended for	Breakfast

'Grab a table outside in the sunshine on a Sunday
morning. Great coffee.'—Theo Randall

LEMONIA

Recommended by
Theo Randall

89 Regent's Park Road
Primrose Hill
London NW1 8UY
+44 2075867454
www.lemonia.co.uk

Opening hours	Open 7 days
Credit cards	Accepted but not AMEX
Price range	Affordable
Style	Casual
Cuisine	Greek
Recommended for	Bargain

'Lovely Greek food, very simple and great value. The octopus salad is always good, as are the grilled sardines.'—Theo Randall

EURO CAFÉ

Recommended by
Martin Morales

45 Sheen Lane
Sheen
London SW14 8AB
+44 2088783535

Opening hours	Open 7 days
Reservation policy	No
Credit cards	Accepted but not AMEX
Price range	Budget
Style	Casual
Cuisine	British
Recommended for	Breakfast

'This place should win the award for best builder's café. It's a guilty pleasure. Value for money, quick, enormous portions, completely relaxing, it's got the whole collection of rubbish tabloid papers on offer every day and it's my local.'—Martin Morales

ABU ZAAD

Recommended by
Sami Tamimi

29 Uxbridge Road
Shepherd's Bush
London W12 8LH
+44 2087495107
www.abuzaad.co.uk

Opening hours	Open 7 days
Credit cards	Accepted but not AMEX
Price range	Budget
Style	Casual
Cuisine	Middle Eastern
Recommended for	Bargain

'This is a fuss-free, family-friendly restaurant serving the best Syrian food in town. It's where I go when I need a Middle Eastern fix. It's busy, pleasantly chaotic and satisfies all my cravings for home and hummus.'
—Sami Tamimi

BIBENDUM

Recommended by
Jeremy Lee

Michelin House
81 Fulham Road
South Kensington
London SW3 6RD
+44 2075815817
www.bibendum.co.uk

Opening hours	Open 7 days
Credit cards	Accepted
Price range	Affordable
Style	Smart casual
Cuisine	French
Recommended for	High end

'Bibendum remains a peerless dining room of great style and it has the most beautiful light. Ravishing. Oysters, Champagne, snails, a *poulet de bresse* and I love diving deep into the wine cellars. It is an extraordinary use of space in an extraordinary building and remains a testament to the great Terence Conran. Just lovely.'—Jeremy Lee

BO LÀNG

Recommended by
Jacob Kenedy

100 Draycott Avenue
South Kensington
London SW3 3AD
+44 2078237887
www.bolangrestaurant.co.uk

Opening hours	Open 7 days
Credit cards	Accepted but not AMEX
Price range	Affordable
Style	Smart casual
Cuisine	Chinese
Recommended for	Breakfast

'Exemplary dim sum.'—Jacob Kenedy

DAQUISE

Recommended by
Rainer Becker

20 Thurloe Street
South Kensington
London SW7 2LT
+44 2075896117
www.daquise.co.uk

Opening hours	Open 7 days
Credit cards	Accepted
Price range	Affordable
Style	Smart casual
Cuisine	Polish
Recommended for	Late night

'It has a unique atmosphere (retro 1950s and 1960s), very traditional service, and tasty Polish food that actually reminds me of my German heritage, which has some similar dishes. You won't find anything else like it in London.'—Rainer Becker

APOLLO BANANA LEAF

Recommended by
Neil Rankin

190 Tooting High Street
Tooting
London SW17 0SF
+44 2086961423
www.apollobananaleaf.com

Opening hours	Open 7 days
Credit cards	Accepted but not AMEX
Price range	Budget
Style	Casual
Cuisine	Sri Lankan
Recommended for	Bargain

'Tooting is, in my opinion, pound for pound the best area for eating out in the whole of the UK... unless you dislike South Indian or Sri Lankan food that is, because that's pretty much all there is. I have about four or five favourites but I've been to Apollo the most and it's a good place to start. Chicken 65 there is the definitive version for me and the mutton roll and devilled mutton are a staple. There are ups and downs but generally the food is spot on and you could eat like a king for less than £15. It's also BYO.'—Neil Rankin

LAHORE KARAHI

Recommended by
Jonathan Jones

1 Tooting High Street
Tooting
London SW17 0SN
+44 2087672477
www.lahorekarahirestaurant.co.uk

Opening hours	Open 7 days
Credit cards	Accepted but not AMEX
Price range	Budget
Style	Casual
Cuisine	Pakistani
Recommended for	Bargain

'Fragrant biryani, smoky bread and good mango lassi.'
—Jonathan Jones

THE LITTLE BAR

145 Mitcham Road
Tooting
London SW17 9PE
+44 2086727317

Opening hours	Open 7 days
Reservation policy	No
Credit cards	Accepted
Price range	Budget
Style	Casual
Cuisine	Bar-Small plates
Recommended for	Wish I'd opened

'Someone's house turned into a wicked little bar. Great drinks and great staff.'—Ollie Couillaud

A.WONG

70 Wilton Road
Victoria
London SW1V 1DE
+44 2078288931
www.awong.co.uk

Recommended by
Jacob Kenedy,
Pierre Koffmann

Opening hours	Closed Sunday
Credit cards	Accepted but not AMEX
Price range	Affordable
Style	Casual
Cuisine	Chinese
Recommended for	Bargain

'Innovative dim sum.'—Pierre Koffmann

CHEZ BRUCE

2 Bellevue Road
Wandsworth
London SW17 7EG
+44 2086720114
www.chezbruce.co.uk

Recommended by
Jeff Galvin,
Marcus Wareing

Opening hours	Open 7 days
Credit cards	Accepted
Price range	Affordable
Style	Smart casual
Cuisine	French
Recommended for	Local favourite

'The food is consistently good, the team are impressive and I have never had a bad meal there. I particularly enjoy the cheese board and talking through the wine list with the sommelier.'—Marcus Wareing

Bruce Poole 'takes it as a compliment' that some find his food old-fashioned. He and Matt Christmas, his kitchen collaborator of ten years, are proud to serve the French-inspired braises, offal dishes, salads and desserts that others eschew. The inspiration is classical, but the style is their own: calf's brains and Puy lentils come with *sauce gribiche* and crisp chicken skin, brandade with mussels and monk's beard, cod with truffle mash and hazelnut dressing. This Wandsworth Common restaurant (twenty-five minutes by cab from town) celebrates two decades in 2015. Its cheeseboard and wine list are now legendary.

BREW

21 High Street
Wimbledon
London SW19 5DX
+44 2089474034
www.brew-cafe.com

Opening hours	Open 7 days
Credit cards	Accepted
Price range	Budget
Style	Casual
Cuisine	Café-Bistro
Recommended for	Breakfast

'The scrambled eggs with chorizo on sourdough is amazing.'—Ollie Couillaud

STICKS'N'SUSHI

58 Wimbledon Hill Road
Wimbledon
London SW19 7PA
+44 2031418800
www.sticksnsushi.com

Opening hours	Open 7 days
Credit cards	Accepted
Price range	Affordable
Style	Casual
Cuisine	Sushi
Recommended for	Regular neighbourhood

'I take my young son who adores it. We always have a great time and the food is mega!'—Ollie Couillaud

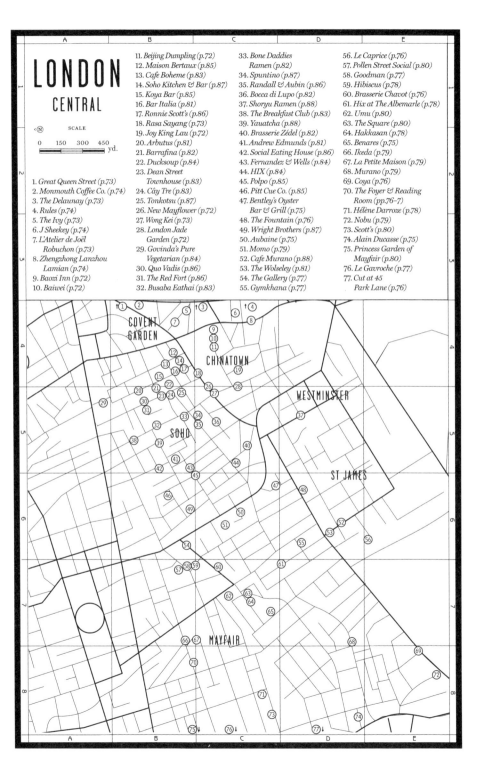

LONDON
CENTRAL

‹N›   SCALE

0   150   300   450
yd.

COVENT GARDEN

CHINATOWN

WESTMINSTER

SOHO

ST JAMES

MAYFAIR

BAIWEI

Recommended by
Stevie Parle

8 Little Newport Street
Chinatown
London WC2H 7JJ
+44 2074943605

Opening hours	Open 7 days
Reservation policy	No
Credit cards	Not accepted
Price range	Budget
Style	Casual
Cuisine	Szechuan
Recommended for	Bargain

'It's extremely high quality and not pretentious.'
—Stevie Parle

BAOZI INN

Recommended by
Jason Atherton, Tom Harris

26 Newport Court
Chinatown
London WC2H 7JS
+44 2072876877
www.baoziinnlondon.com

Opening hours	Open 7 days
Reservation policy	No
Credit cards	Not accepted
Price range	Budget
Style	Casual
Cuisine	Chinese
Recommended for	Bargain

'They serve a whole, deeply savoury, porky meatball in a soft, fluffy steamed bun. It's good. This is Chinese street food at its finest transferred to the streets of London.'—Tom Harris

BEIJING DUMPLING

Recommended by
Giorgio Locatelli

23 Lisle Street
Chinatown
London WC2H 7BA
+44 2072876888

Opening hours	Open 7 days
Credit cards	Accepted but not AMEX
Price range	Budget
Style	Casual
Cuisine	Chinese
Recommended for	Late night

'Fantastic hand-made dumplings that must be the tastiest in Chinatown.'—Giorgio Locatelli

JOY KING LAU

Recommended by
Matthew Harris

3 Leicester Street
Chinatown
London WC2H 7BL
+44 2074371132
www.joykinglau.com

Opening hours	Open 7 days
Credit cards	Accepted
Price range	Budget
Style	Casual
Cuisine	Cantonese
Recommended for	Bargain

'Great, cheap dim sum.'—Matthew Harris

LONDON JADE GARDEN

Recommended by
Fergus Henderson

15 Wardour Street
Chinatown
London W1D 6PH
+44 2074375065
www.londonjadegarden.com

Opening hours	Open 7 days
Credit cards	Accepted
Price range	Budget
Style	Casual
Cuisine	Chinese
Recommended for	Bargain

'Dim sum yum!'—Fergus Henderson

NEW MAYFLOWER

Recommended by
Alexis Gauthier

68–70 Shaftesbury Avenue
Chinatown
London W1D 6LY
+44 2077349207
www.newmayflowerlondon.com

Opening hours	Open 7 days
Credit cards	Accepted but not AMEX
Price range	Budget
Style	Casual
Cuisine	Chinese
Recommended for	Late night

'Consistent, and good service.'—Alexis Gauthier

RASA SAYANG

Recommended by
Mitch Tonks

5 Macclesfield Street
Chinatown
London W1D 6AY
+44 2077341382
www.rasasayangfood.com

Opening hours	Open 7 days
Credit cards	Accepted
Price range	Budget
Style	Casual
Cuisine	Malaysian
Recommended for	Bargain

'Really good quality Malaysian curry and you can feast
very, very well for under £10.'—Mitch Tonks

WONG KEI

Recommended by
Ollie Couillaud

41–43 Wardour Street
Chinatown
London W1D 6PY
+44 2074378408
www.wongkeilondon.com

Opening hours	Open 7 days
Reservation policy	No
Credit cards	Not accepted
Price range	Budget
Style	Casual
Cuisine	Chinese
Recommended for	Late night

'For when you're drunk and hungry at 3.00 or 4.00 a.m.'
—Ollie Couillaud

L'ATELIER DE JOËL ROBUCHON

Recommended by
Bo Bech, Heinz
Beck, Ebbe Vollmer

13–15 West Street
Covent Garden
London WC2H 9NE
+44 2070108600
www.joelrobuchon.co.uk

Opening hours	Open 7 days
Credit cards	Accepted
Price range	Expensive
Style	Smart casual
Cuisine	Modern French
Recommended for	High end

THE DELAUNAY

Recommended by
Angela Hartnett,
Karam Sethi

55 Aldwych
Covent Garden
London WC2B 4BB
+44 2074998558
www.thedelaunay.com

Opening hours	Open 7 days
Credit cards	Accepted
Price range	Affordable
Style	Smart casual
Cuisine	European
Recommended for	Breakfast

'I just love the food. I usually go for a full English or the
Viennese breakfast.'—Karam Sethi

GREAT QUEEN STREET

Recommended by
Tom Pemberton

32 Great Queen Street
Covent Garden
London WC2B 5AA
+44 2072420622
www.greatqueenstreetrestaurant.co.uk

Opening hours	Open 7 days
Credit cards	Accepted but not AMEX
Price range	Affordable
Style	Casual
Cuisine	British
Recommended for	Bargain

'Tasty and reasonably priced.'—Tom Pemberton

THE IVY

Recommended by
Dominic Chapman, Alexis
Gauthier, Matthew Harris,
Ilya Shalev

1–5 West Street
Covent Garden
London WC2H 9NQ
+44 2078364751
www.the-ivy.co.uk

Opening hours	Open 7 days
Credit cards	Accepted
Price range	Affordable
Style	Smart casual
Cuisine	Modern European
Recommended for	Local favourite

'Super service and a sense of occasion, even if you
just order a shepherd's pie. They serve well-prepared
classics. There is a reason why this restaurant is full
every night, and has been forever.'—Alexis Gauthier

J SHEEKEY

28–35 St Martin's Court
Covent Garden
London WC2N 4AL
+44 2072402565
www.j-sheekey.co.uk

Recommended by
Pascal Aussignac,
Thomasina Miers, Ben Tish

Opening hours	Open 7 days
Credit cards	Accepted
Price range	Affordable
Style	Smart casual
Cuisine	Seafood
Recommended for	High end

'It's my favourite restaurant in town. Decadent and unpretentious all at once. The food is always consistently amazing and, refreshingly, it never follows trends. The whole turbot for two with a bottle of Champagne is as good as it gets for me.'—Ben Tish

MONMOUTH COFFEE COMPANY

27 Monmouth Street
Covent Garden
London WC2H 9EU
+44 2072323010
www.monmouthcoffee.co.uk

Recommended by
Mikael Jonsson

Opening hours	Closed Sunday
Reservation policy	No
Credit cards	Accepted but not AMEX
Price range	Budget
Style	Casual
Cuisine	Coffee Shop
Recommended for	Breakfast

'The coffee is great.'—Mikael Jonsson

RULES

35 Maiden Lane
Covent Garden
London WC2E 7LB
+44 2078365314
www.rules.co.uk

Recommended by
Ben Tish

Opening hours	Open 7 days
Credit cards	Accepted
Price range	Expensive
Style	Smart casual
Cuisine	British
Recommended for	Local favourite

'Sums up our city's food heritage. It's one of London's oldest restaurants and serves expertly cooked braises and old-school pies. It recently had a revamp and the upstairs bar now serves some serious cocktails. A hidden gem.'—Ben Tish

ZHENGZHONG LANZHOU LAMIAN

33 Cranbourn Street
Covent Garden
London WC2H 7AD
+44 2078364399

Recommended by
Martin Morales

Opening hours	Open 7 days
Credit cards	Not accepted
Price range	Budget
Style	Casual
Cuisine	Chinese
Recommended for	Late night

'You can watch the world go by while eating freshly made noodles and great broth.'—Martin Morales

ALAIN DUCASSE

Recommended by
Olivier Limousin, Clare
Smyth, Marcus Wareing

The Dorchester
53 Park Lane
Mayfair
London W1K 1QA
+44 2076298866
www.alainducasse-dorchester.com

Opening hours	Closed Monday and Sunday
Credit cards	Accepted
Price range	Expensive
Style	Smart casual
Cuisine	Modern French
Recommended for	High end

'It got knocked a lot when Chef Jocelyn earned two Michelin stars so soon after opening. However, having recently visited, I thought the service and food were both superb and well worth the three Michelin stars that they now have. The little extras and manager Nicolas really make it a very special experience.'
—Marcus Wareing

AUBAINE

Recommended by
Olivier Limousin

4 Heddon Street
Mayfair
London W1B 4BS
+44 2074402510
www.aubaine.co.uk

Opening hours	Open 7 days
Credit cards	Accepted
Price range	Affordable
Style	Casual
Cuisine	French Bistro
Recommended for	Breakfast

'Every time I have friends visiting me, I always go to Aubaine. The viennoiserie and bread are very nice. I like the decoration too – it looks like you are in the south of France, and there's always good service.'
—Olivier Limousin

BENARES

Recommended by
Bryn Williams

12a Berkeley Square House
Berkeley Square
Mayfair
London W1J 6BS
+44 2076298886
www.benaresrestaurant.com

Opening hours	Closed Sunday
Credit cards	Accepted
Price range	Expensive
Style	Smart casual
Cuisine	Modern Indian
Recommended for	High end

BENTLEY'S OYSTER BAR & GRILL

Recommended by
Nigel Haworth,
Thomasina Miers,
Bryn Williams

11–15 Swallow Street
Mayfair
London W1B 4DG
+44 2077344756
www.bentleys.org

Opening hours	Open 7 days
Credit cards	Accepted
Price range	Expensive
Style	Smart casual
Cuisine	Seafood-Grill
Recommended for	Wish I'd opened

Irish chef Richard Corrigan rebuilt the reputation of this most English of restaurants when he took it over and refurbished it in 2005. First opened in 1916, a classic West End oyster bar and grill, located on a cut-through between Regent's Street and Piccadilly, it now consists of an upper floor grill, where meat sits alongside the fish, and a street level oyster bar. The latter, where marble counter meets red leather upholstery at bar and booth, and seasoned old oyster campaigners in white jackets do their shucking, is a jewel. Outside, a large swathe of Swallow Street does al fresco dining.

BRASSERIE CHAVOT

41 Conduit Street
Mayfair
London W1S 2YF
+44 2071836425
www.brasseriechavot.com

Recommended by
Tom Aikens,
Alyn Williams

Opening hours	Open 7 days
Credit cards	Accepted
Price range	Affordable
Style	Casual
Cuisine	French Brasserie
Recommended for	Wish I'd opened

'Fantastic restaurant. Chef Eric Chavot immediately hit the ground running – considering he was out of the UK for a number of years, he certainly has not lost his touch.'
—Tom Aikens

LE CAPRICE

Arlington House
Arlington Street
Mayfair
London SW1A 1RJ
+44 2076292239
www.le-caprice.co.uk

Recommended by
Thomasina Miers

Opening hours	Open 7 days
Credit cards	Accepted
Price range	Expensive
Style	Smart casual
Cuisine	Modern European
Recommended for	Late night

COYA

118 Piccadilly
Mayfair
London W1J 7NW
+44 2070427118
www.coyarestaurant.com

Recommended by
André Jaeger

Opening hours	Open 7 days
Credit cards	Accepted
Price range	Affordable
Style	Smart casual
Cuisine	Peruvian
Recommended for	Worth the travel

'Peruvian is a cuisine not really known to us. I had a wonderful and most satisfying lunch here. I was impressed by the ease of the service, the taste and quality of the food. I think this is a restaurant concept with great potential.'—André Jaeger

CUT AT 45 PARK LANE

45 Park Lane
Mayfair
London W1K 1PN
+44 2074934554
www.45parklane.com/CUTat45ParkLane

Recommended by
Francesco Mazzei,
Agnar Sverrisson

Opening hours	Open 7 days
Credit cards	Accepted
Price range	Expensive
Style	Smart casual
Cuisine	Steakhouse
Recommended for	High end

'I like to go to CUT at Park Lane for an early brunch.'
—Agnar Sverrisson

THE FOUNTAIN

Fortnum & Mason
181 Piccadilly
Mayfair
London W1A 1ER
+44 8453001707
www.fortnumandmason.com

Recommended by
Shaun Hill

Opening hours	Open 7 days
Credit cards	Accepted
Price range	Affordable
Style	Smart casual
Cuisine	British
Recommended for	Breakfast

'Simple things done well in very snazzy surrounds. Breakfast is not the moment for industrial architecture and cutting-edge grub. Good Eggs Benedict and freshly made coffee served by polite and efficient people is the order of the day.'—Shaun Hill

THE FOYER & READING ROOM

Claridge's
Brook Street
Mayfair
London W1K 4HR
+44 2071078886
www.claridges.co.uk

Recommended by
Adam Byatt,
Jeff Galvin

Opening hours	Open 7 days
Credit cards	Accepted
Price range	Expensive
Style	Smart casual
Cuisine	British
Recommended for	Local favourite

'I go for afternoon tea. It feels incredibly London – sophisticated, generous and so well put together. A real treat and an institution.'—Adam Byatt

THE GALLERY

Sketch
9 Conduit Street
Mayfair
London W1S 2XG
+44 2076594500
www.sketch.uk.com

Recommended by
Pascal Aussignac, Ettore
Botrini, Marcus Eaves, Jeff
Galvin, Sergio Herman

Opening hours	Open 7 days
Credit cards	Accepted
Price range	Expensive
Style	Smart casual
Cuisine	Modern European
Recommended for	Late night

'There is only one restaurant I wished was mine and that is Sketch in London. It has been around for years but every time I'm there it's like I am discovering it all over again! The place bursts with creativity with all of its different concepts and is a total experience for all the senses.'—Sergio Herman

Mourad Mazouz's operation with partner Pierre Gagnaire, opened in 2003, remains the most bizarrely ambitious ever-evolving bar/restaurant/gallery/nightclub that London – perhaps anywhere – has ever seen. For pure fun forget the fine-dining opulence of The Lecture Room and head downstairs to The Gallery instead. Dramatically transformed in mid-2012 to a design courtesy of celebrated Scottish artist Martin Creed, the artfully mix-matched furniture, brightly tiled floor and patterned walls have since been replaced by India Mahdavi's plush bourgeois fittings and powder-pink walls lined with British artist David Shrigley's original drawings. The plan is for a different artist to redesign the room every year or so. Gagnaire's ever-wacky menu continues to mix luxury, comfort and creativity.

LE GAVROCHE

43 Upper Brook Street
Mayfair
London W1K 7QR
+44 2074080881
www.le-gavroche.co.uk

Recommended by
Chris Galvin, Jeff Galvin,
Henry Harris, Fergus
Henderson, Pierre Koffmann,
Paul Owens, Clare Smyth,
Bryn Williams

Opening hours	Closed Sunday
Credit cards	Accepted
Price range	Expensive
Style	Smart casual
Cuisine	French
Recommended for	High end

'You feel stroked inside and out.'—Fergus Henderson

GOODMAN

26 Maddox Street
Mayfair
London W1S 1QH
+44 2074993776
www.goodmanrestaurants.com

Recommended by
Jason Atherton

Opening hours	Closed Sunday
Credit cards	Accepted
Price range	Affordable
Style	Smart casual
Cuisine	Steakhouse
Recommended for	Late night

GYMKHANA

42 Albemarle Street
Mayfair
London W1S 4JH
+44 2030115900
www.gymkhanalondon.com

Recommended by
Stevie Parle, Neil Rankin

Opening hours	Closed Sunday
Credit cards	Accepted
Price range	Affordable
Style	Smart casual
Cuisine	Modern Indian
Recommended for	Regular neighbourhood

'There is nothing I dislike about this restaurant. Indian food is hands down my favourite food to eat and here is a place that not only does it with impeccable skill and using the best ingredients, but they also have a great wine and cocktail list. And they have created a space that I would happily move into and never leave. The food menu is such that you never get bored as everything sounds great and almost all of it delivers.' —Neil Rankin

HAKKASAN

17 Bruton Street
Mayfair
London W1J 6QB
+44 2079071888
www.hakkasan.com

Recommended by
Galton Blackiston, Alberto
Chicote, Gert de Mangeleer,
André Garrett, Philip Howard,
Francesco Mazzei, Agnar
Sverrisson, Martin Wishart

Opening hours	Open 7 days
Credit cards	Accepted
Price range	Expensive
Style	Smart casual
Cuisine	Modern Chinese
Recommended for	Late night

'Glamorous, delicious and there's always a buzz.'
—Philip Howard

HÉLÈNE DARROZE

The Connaught
Carlos Place
Mayfair
London W1K 2AL
+44 2071078880
www.the-connaught.co.uk

Recommended by
Tom Aikens

Opening hours	Closed Monday and Sunday
Credit cards	Accepted
Price range	Expensive
Style	Formal
Cuisine	Modern French
Recommended for	High end

'A beautiful space which always feels very special.'
—Tom Aikens

The Connaught has seen many fine chefs and France's culinary queen Hélène Darroze is the latest to weave her magic in this historic Mayfair hotel. Her native Landes in southwest France is name-checked several times on the menu: terrine of foie gras from les Landes; corn-fed chicken from les Landes... And she cleverly introduces her native cuisine into her take on the American brunch, served on Saturdays from 11.00 a.m. Charcuterie, terrines and Périgord truffles join smoked salmon, York ham and hot dogs, all in the most stylish and refined of circumstances, of course.

HIBISCUS

29 Maddox Street
Mayfair
London W1S 2PA
+44 2076292999
www.hibiscusrestaurant.co.uk

Recommended by
Clare Smyth

Opening hours	Closed Sunday
Credit cards	Accepted
Price range	Expensive
Style	Smart casual
Cuisine	Modern French
Recommended for	Worth the travel

It was a brave decision after seven successful years in rural Shropshire to move Hibiscus to metropolitan Mayfair. But since successfully transplanting Hibiscus from Ludlow to London back in 2007, Lyon-born Claude Bosi's reputation as a purveyor of forward-thinking haute cuisine has soared and he's had no reason to look back. The kitchen is discreetly hidden behind a set of swish sliding doors, which open onto an intimate oak-panelled dining room, where the focus is on polished service and Bosi's ever-evolving modern French menus that trawl the British Isles for raw materials and the globe for inspiration.

HIX AT THE ALBEMARLE

Brown's Hotel
Albemarle Street
Mayfair
London W1S 4BP
+44 2075184004
www.hixmayfair.co.uk

Recommended by
Atul Kochhar

Opening hours	Open 7 days
Credit cards	Accepted
Price range	Expensive
Style	Smart casual
Cuisine	British
Recommended for	Late night

'Mark Hix is a great chef for reinventing and reimagining British food.'—Atul Kochar

IKEDA

Recommended by
Margot Henderson

30 Brook Street
Mayfair
London W1K 5DJ
+44 2076292730
www.ikedarestaurant.com

Opening hours...Closed Sunday
Credit cards..Accepted
Price range..Expensive
Style..Smart casual
Cuisine..Japanese
Recommended for...High end

MOMO

Recommended by
Theo Randall

25 Heddon Street
Mayfair
London W1B 4BH
+44 2074344040
www.momoresto.com

Opening hours..Open 7 days
Credit cards..Accepted
Price range...Affordable
Style..Smart casual
Cuisine..Moroccan
Recommended for...Late night

'Great tagine and cous cous, with a dance in the bar afterwards a must.'—Theo Randall

MURANO

Recommended by
José Pizarro

20 Queen Street
Mayfair
London W1J 5PP
+44 2074951127
www.muranolondon.com

Opening hours...Closed Sunday
Credit cards..Accepted
Price range..Expensive
Style..Smart casual
Cuisine..Italian
Recommended for...High end

'I just love Angela's food. Good food handled simply and with great care.'—José Pizarro

NOBU

Recommended by
Ricardo Zarate

Metropolitan Hotel
19 Old Park Lane
Mayfair
London W1K 1LB
+44 2074474747
www.noburestaurants.com/london

Opening hours..Open 7 days
Credit cards..Accepted
Price range..Expensive
Style..Smart casual
Cuisine..Modern Japanese
Recommended for...Worth the travel

LA PETITE MAISON

Recommended by
Tom Kitchin, Olivier
Limousin, Theo Randall,
Karam Sethi, Mitch Tonks

53–54 Brook's Mews
Mayfair
London W1K 4EG
+44 2074954774
www.lpmlondon.co.uk

Opening hours..Open 7 days
Credit cards..Accepted
Price range...Affordable
Style..Smart casual
Cuisine..Niçoise
Recommended for..Wish I'd opened

'I have huge admiration for my dear friend Raphael Duntoye, the chef behind La Petite Maison and the Arts Club in London. He is a fantastically talented chef. La Petite Maison is probably my favourite restaurant in London. I just love the clean cooking and his fantastic ways of mixing flavours.'—Tom Kitchin

This offshoot of the famous Nice hotspot of the same name (Sarkozy is said to be a fan) caters for its similarly starry regulars and the Mayfair set by combining a luxuriously bourgeois French menu with suave but informal service. Dishes are designed for sharing and arrive at the table in their own time, from hors d'oeuvres to rich comforting mains such as truffled macaroni and Mediterranean classics such as salt-baked sea bass. If there's a dish that sums up the whole experience, it's probably the whole Black Leg chicken stuffed with foie gras – roasted to order and well worth the hour's wait.

POLLEN STREET SOCIAL

Recommended by
Tom Kerridge

8–10 Pollen Street
Mayfair
London W1S 1NQ
+44 2072907600
www.pollenstreetsocial.com

Opening hours	Closed Sunday
Credit cards	Accepted
Price range	Expensive
Style	Smart casual
Cuisine	Modern British
Recommended for	Wish I'd opened

'Consistently hits that balance between high-end cuisine, funky fun atmosphere, and a great bar.'
—Tom Kerridge

PRINCESS GARDEN OF MAYFAIR

Recommended by
Theo Randall

8–10 North Audley Street
Mayfair
London W1K 6ZD
+44 2074933223
www.princessgardenofmayfair.com

Opening hours	Open 7 days
Credit cards	Accepted
Price range	Affordable
Style	Smart casual
Cuisine	Chinese
Recommended for	Regular neighbourhood

'Fantastic dim sum, great for a big-table Sunday lunch.'
—Theo Randall

SCOTT'S

Recommended by
Philip Howard, Clare Smyth,
Marcus Wareing

20 Mount Street
Mayfair
London W1K 2HE
+44 2074957309
www.scotts-restaurant.com

Opening hours	Open 7 days
Credit cards	Accepted
Price range	Expensive
Style	Smart casual
Cuisine	Seafood
Recommended for	Wish I'd opened

'I love the decor and the consistent menu – I just wish it was mine!'—Marcus Wareing

THE SQUARE

Recommended by
Neil Borthwick, Adam Byatt,
Ollie Couillaud, Chris Galvin,
Sam Harris, Angela Hartnett,
Hywel Jones, Bruce Poole

6–10 Bruton Street
Mayfair
London W1J 6PU
+44 2074957100
www.squarerestaurant.com

Opening hours	Open 7 days
Credit cards	Accepted
Price range	Expensive
Style	Smart casual
Cuisine	Modern French
Recommended for	High end

'Just total class, and such consistency after so many years. The wine list is one of the best in London, and the over-sized tables for two give an almost regal effect.'—Sam Harris

Now in its third decade, The Square has earned itself a reputation as a perennial source of high-quality fine dining in the heart of Mayfair. Chef patron Philip Howard and head chef Gary Foulkes specialize in taking seasonal and predominantly British ingredients such as Dover sole, prawns and ox cheeks, and applying a twist of French flair that transforms them into sophisticated yet refreshingly unfussy dishes that are simply delicious. A menu like this deserves a stonking good wine list and in this respect The Square doesn't disappoint.

UMU

Recommended by
Ollie Dabbous

14–16 Bruton Place
Mayfair
London W1J 6LX
+44 2074998881
www.umurestaurant.com

Opening hours	Closed Sunday
Credit cards	Accepted
Price range	Expensive
Style	Smart casual
Cuisine	Japanese
Recommended for	High end

THE WOLSELEY

160 Piccadilly
Mayfair
London W1J 9EB
+44 2074996996
www.thewolseley.com

Recommended by
Tom Aikens, Jason Atherton,
Dominic Chapman, Marcus
Eaves, Chris Galvin, André
Garrett, Steffen Hansen,
Matthew Harris, Nigel
Haworth, Philip Howard, Atul
Kochhar, Francesco Mazzei,
Tom Oldroyd, José Pizarro,
Bruce Poole, Ruth Rogers,
Karam Sethi, Ilya Shalev, Sami
Tamimi, Peter Weeden, Alyn
Williams, Bryn Williams

Opening hours...Open 7 days
Credit cards...Accepted
Price range...Expensive
Style...Smart casual
Cuisine...European
Recommended for..Breakfast

'The space is great – the combination of London heritage with Viennese café grandeur transports you to the 1920s and feels a long way from the streets of Piccadilly outside. The food is classic, comforting and reliable: always a good way to start the day. The breakfast menu has something for everyone – oysters, scrambled eggs, apple strudel, a simple croissant. I always have the kedgeree and kippers with mustard butter.'
—Sami Tamimi

Such is its overwhelmingly popularity as a breakfast venue, many of its loyal regulars never go to The Wolseley for either lunch or dinner, although it's typically full for both. The lengthy morning menu is packed with comfort: crumpets, kedgeree, crispy bacon rolls, Eggs Benedict, fried haggis with duck eggs, Omelette Arnold Bennett and a fine selection of Viennese pastries – to name but a fraction of what's on offer. But it's also about the setting and the sumptuous space. Once the Piccadilly showroom for the old marque it's named after, it's now a sweeping grand café in the European style.

ANDREW EDMUNDS

46 Lexington Street
Soho
London W1F 0LP
+44 2074375708
www.andrewedmunds.com

Recommended by
James Knappett

Opening hours...Open 7 days
Credit cards...............................Accepted but not AMEX
Price range...Affordable
Style...Smart casual
Cuisine..Bistro
Recommended for...Bargain

ARBUTUS

63–64 Frith Street
Soho
London W1D 3JW
+44 2077344545
www.arbutusrestaurant.co.uk

Recommended by
André Garrett

Opening hours...Open 7 days
Credit cards...Accepted
Price range...Affordable
Style..Casual
Cuisine..Bistro
Recommended for...Bargain

'Great price and a tasty lunch menu.'—André Garrett

BAR ITALIA

22 Frith Street
Soho
London W1D 4RF
+44 2074374520
www.baritaliasoho.co.uk

Recommended by
Chris Galvin, Margot
Henderson, Tom Oldroyd,
Alfred Prasad

Opening hours...Open 7 days
Reservation policy..No
Credit cards...............................Accepted but not AMEX
Price range...Affordable
Style..Casual
Cuisine...Coffee Shop
Recommended for...Late night

'I love its classic Italian café look, its bustling energy and the sense of community. You see all sorts of characters there, which just adds to the charm of this legendary café. I love their tiramisù, coffee and friendliness. Great place to wrap up a night out.'
—Alfred Prasad

BARRAFINA

54 Frith Street
Soho
London W1D 4SL
www.barrafina.co.uk

Recommended by
Jason Atherton, Robin Gill,
Angela Hartnett, Margot
Henderson, Adam Stokes

Opening hours	Open 7 days
Reservation policy	No
Credit cards	Accepted
Price range	Affordable
Style	Casual
Cuisine	Tapas
Recommended for	Regular neighbourhood

'Nieves and head chef Jose rule Spanish food in London. I love the sardines a la plancha and gambas aioli.'—Angela Hartnett

The Hart brothers' tribute to Barcelona's legendary Cal Pep consists of only twenty-three stools around a marble counter. The crammed open kitchen behind it produces top-class tapas, from grilled meat and game, to seafood cooked a la plancha. Throw in an excellent all-Iberian wine list and good-natured service that deals efficiently and politely with the inevitable waiting throng come peak times. Relax, grab a draught of cold Cruzcampo or two and a plate of *jamón* while you wait, and watch Soho go by.

BOCCA DI LUPO

12 Archer Street
Soho
London W1D 7BB
+44 2077342223
www.boccadilupo.com

Recommended by
Thomasina Miers

Opening hours	Open 7 days
Credit cards	Accepted
Price range	Affordable
Style	Casual
Cuisine	Italian
Recommended for	Regular neighbourhood

BONE DADDIES RAMEN BAR

31 Peter Street
Soho
London W1F 0AR
+44 2072878581
www.bonedaddiesramen.com

Recommended by
Adam Byatt, Miles Kirby,
Peter Weeden

Opening hours	Open 7 days
Reservation policy	No
Credit cards	Accepted
Price range	Budget
Style	Casual
Cuisine	Ramen Noodles
Recommended for	Late night

'Ramen heaven.'—Miles Kirby

Despite the unmarked facade, this NYC-style ramen bar isn't high on subtlety: diners are barraged with rock music and images of Japanese rockabillies, while menu options such as Cock Scratchings and swift service mean it's probably not a place to take a parent or a date. The cooking, helmed by ex-Zuma and ex-Nobu head chef Ross Shonhan, is just as punchy, with rich takes on classics like *tonkotsu* ramen — with its twenty-hour simmered pork bones — packing a serious amount of flavour for the price. A good list of sake, shochu and whisky keeps the young Soho crowd happy.

BRASSERIE ZÉDEL

20 Sherwood Street
Soho
London W1F 7ED
+44 2077344888
www.brasseriezedel.com

Recommended by
Ben Tish

Opening hours	Open 7 days
Credit cards	Accepted
Price range	Affordable
Style	Smart casual
Cuisine	French Brasserie
Recommended for	Late night

'It's a very central location so it's a great place to go after drinks in Soho. Always tasty and delicious – the steak tartare and chips is good – and it's no nonsense, the service is quick and it's unbelievable value for money. There's also a great bar next door if you fancy another.'—Ben Tish

THE BREAKFAST CLUB

Recommended by
Adam Stokes

33 D'Arblay Street
Soho
London W1F 8EU
+44 2074342571
www.thebreakfastclubcafes.com

Opening hours	Open 7 days
Credit cards	Accepted but not AMEX
Price range	Budget
Style	Casual
Cuisine	Café-Bistro
Recommended for	Breakfast

'Cool and quirky. Great sausages and duck eggs.'
—Adam Stokes

BUSABA EATHAI

Recommended by
Omar Allibhoy, Pascal
Aussignac, Atul Kochhar,
Francesco Mazzei,
Agnar Sverrisson

106–110 Wardour Street
Soho
London W1F 0TR
+44 2072558686
www.busaba.com

Opening hours	Open 7 days
Reservation policy	No
Credit cards	Accepted
Price range	Budget
Style	Casual
Cuisine	Thai
Recommended for	Bargain

'Lovely Thai flavours, great value for money and very
quick and efficient service.'—Agnar Sverrisson

CAFE BOHEME

Recommended by
Olivier Limousin

13 Old Compton Street
Soho
London W1D 5JQ
+44 2077340623
www.cafeboheme.co.uk

Opening hours	Open 7 days
Credit cards	Accepted
Price range	Affordable
Style	Casual
Cuisine	French Bistro
Recommended for	Late night

'Always busy with a fun vibe and good food.'
—Olivier Limousin

CÂY TRE

Recommended by
Alexis Gauthier,
Stevie Parle

42–43 Dean Street
Soho
London W1D 4PZ
+44 2073179118
www.caytresoho.co.uk

Opening hours	Open 7 days
Credit cards	Accepted
Price range	Budget
Style	Casual
Cuisine	Vietnamese
Recommended for	Bargain

'For Vietnamese food this place is hard to beat. Very
fresh ingredients, varied menu and extremely good
value. I go a lot.'—Alexis Gauthier

DEAN STREET TOWNHOUSE

Recommended by
Alexis Gauthier,
Tom Oldroyd

69–71 Dean Street
Soho
London W1D 3SE
+44 2074341775
www.deanstreettownhouse.com

Opening hours	Open 7 days
Credit cards	Accepted
Price range	Affordable
Style	Smart casual
Cuisine	British
Recommended for	Breakfast

'Great buzzy atmosphere, not too stuffy and always
good food.'—Alexis Gauthier

This handsome Georgian townhouse in the heart of
Soho has seen some action over the years, notably
as the Gargoyle club, a louche drinking den frequented
by arty souls such as Francis Bacon and Lucian Freud.
Since then its various parts have been a snooker club
and a sauna, and most recently it was a branch of
a grim pub chain. It suits its latest role as a stylish
Soho House-operated boutique hotel with an all-day
dining room doing simple British food. It's a luxuriously
relaxed place to start the day, the menu offering
everything from baskets of pastries to Manx kippers.

DUCKSOUP

Recommended by
Margot Henderson, Miles
Kirby, Sami Tamimi

41 Dean Street
Soho
London W1D 4PY
+44 2072874599
www.ducksoupsoho.co.uk

Opening hours	Open 7 days
Reservation policy	No
Credit cards	Accepted
Price range	Affordable
Style	Casual
Cuisine	European small plates
Recommended for	Regular neighbourhood

'It's a small place with a long bar. The decor is pared down – white tiles, bare lights – with the focus, instead, on great food. The plates are for sharing and they have the confidence to let the ingredients do the talking. No frills or foams! The wines are really interesting too: there's a focus on natural wines, which you can have by the glass.'—Sami Tamimi

FERNANDEZ & WELLS

Recommended by
Yotam Ottolenghi

73 Beak Street
Soho
London W1F 9SR
+44 2072878124
www.fernandezandwells.com

Opening hours	Open 7 days
Reservation policy	No
Credit cards	Accepted
Price range	Budget
Style	Casual
Cuisine	Café-Bar-Bistro
Recommended for	Breakfast

'The coffee is exceptionally good. It's also a place where I can justify eating an *jamón ibérico* and tomato sandwich before midday.'—Yotam Ottolenghi

GOVINDA'S PURE VEGETARIAN

Recommended by
Tom Oldroyd

Radha-Krishna Temple
10 Soho Street
Soho
London W1D 3DL
+44 2074405229
www.iskcon-london.org/visiting/govinda-s-restaurant

Opening hours	Open 7 days
Credit cards	Accepted
Price range	Budget
Style	Casual
Cuisine	Vegetarian
Recommended for	Bargain

'Although I will probably live to regret letting you in on this, the Hare Krishna temple just off Soho Square offers up some of the tastiest cheap eats in Central London.'—Tom Oldroyd

HIX

Recommended by
Angela Hartnett, Thomasina
Miers, Manoj Vasaikar

66–70 Brewer Street
Soho
London W1F 9UP
+44 2072923518
www.hixsoho.co.uk

Opening hours	Open 7 days
Credit cards	Accepted
Price range	Affordable
Style	Smart casual
Cuisine	British
Recommended for	Late night

'Very casual food with substance and good wine. Lots of seasonal produce used.'—Manoj Vasaikar

Mark Hix's Soho flagship, like the man himself, is often at its best late at night. The buzz of the street-level dining room tends to crescendo until it closes, by which time there is the basement bar and its cocktail menu in which to take refuge. The simple British seasonal approach of the kitchen is applied to everything from shellfish to steaks. The informal ambience is arguably a double-edged sword – while you'll feel comfortable enough to eat a late-night dinner here after a few too many, so does everyone else. But then who comes here for a quiet dinner?

KOYA BAR

50 Frith Street
Soho
London W1D 4SQ
www.koyabar.co.uk

Recommended by
James Lowe

Opening hours	Open 7 days
Reservation policy	No
Credit cards	Accepted but not AMEX
Price range	Budget
Style	Casual
Cuisine	Japanese
Recommended for	Breakfast

'The newest addition to one of the best restaurants in London is this bar-restaurant next door to the original [now closed] Koya. It features the udon and fabulous stocks that have made Koya such a favourite, as well as things like kedgeree porridge and bacon and egg udon at breakfast time.'—James Lowe

MAISON BERTAUX

28 Greek Street
Soho
London W1D 5DQ
+44 2074376007
www.maisonbertaux.com

Recommended by
Jeremy Lee

Opening hours	Open 7 days
Reservation policy	No
Credit cards	Accepted
Price range	Budget
Style	Casual
Cuisine	French Patisserie
Recommended for	Breakfast

'I have been eating here since a dim and distant youth. They are the best in London.'—Jeremy Lee

This old Soho spot boasts of being London's oldest patisserie, originally opened by Communards who, having fled Paris following the failure of the Fourth French Revolution, took refuge in cake. While it's true that the service can be hit and miss, it never fails to be entertainingly theatrical. The French fancies and cream cakes, still baked daily on the premises, are a reliable source of calories and le café au lait 'c'est bon'. Whether it's from a window table at street level or out on the pavement, there are few better vantage points from which to watch Soho go by.

PITT CUE CO.

1 Newburgh Street
Soho
London W1F 7RB
www.pittcue.co.uk

Recommended by
Marcus Eaves,
James Lowe

Opening hours	Open 7 days
Reservation policy	No
Credit cards	Accepted
Price range	Affordable
Style	Casual
Cuisine	Barbeque
Recommended for	Bargain

'Not a cheap restaurant exactly but it's definitely the number-one bargain in town. It has an unrivalled commitment to serving the best barbeque, beer and bourbon around.'—Marcus Eaves

Following a successful summer residency operating out of a van on the South Bank, the Pitt Cue Co. made these bijou premises off Carnaby Street their permanent home. Head here for a late lunch early in the week to avoid the queues for a stool in the pint-sized bar or to grab a table in their basement bunker of a dining room. Chef Tom Adams's skill with a smoker, combined with the sourcing of the perfect cuts of pork and beef, make for a carnivores' Shangri-La. A short list of craft beers, ciders and bourbon-based cocktails provide the liquid refreshment.

POLPO

41 Beak Street
Soho
London W1F 9SB
+44 2077344479
www.polpo.co.uk

Recommended by
Marcus Eaves, Shaun
Hill, Bryn Williams

Opening hours	Open 7 days
Reservation policy	No
Credit cards	Accepted
Price range	Affordable
Style	Casual
Cuisine	Italian small plates
Recommended for	Wish I'd opened

'I'm a massive fan of this place and its emphasis on simply great food in a chilled-out, stripped-back environment. Polpo opened in 2009 and it's still one of the hottest tables in London.'—Marcus Eaves

QUO VADIS

26–29 Dean Street
Soho
London W1D 3LL
+44 2074379585
www.quovadissoho.co.uk

Recommended by
Tom Adams, Tom Oldroyd,
José Pizarro

Opening hours	Closed Sunday
Credit cards	Accepted
Price range	Affordable
Style	Smart casual
Cuisine	British
Recommended for	Regular neighbourhood

'From menu to mouth, this restaurant never fails to deliver. I am yet to have a bad experience there. The slick, friendly and attentive service sets the scene in which Jeremy Lee's timeless cooking is readily received.'—Tom Oldroyd

The arrival in 2011 of Jeremy Lee at Quo Vadis, after years at the Blueprint Café, breathed new life into the old Soho landmark that's been running as a restaurant since 1929. He has a smart, seasonal way with British produce and remains one of the best cooks of game in London, if not the country. Trademark dishes include baked salsify wrapped in phyllo pastry and topped with grated Parmesan, a smoked eel and horseradish sandwich and the classic Elizabeth David dessert – although Lee prefers to talk about 'puddings' – St Emilion au chocolat. The 'Theatre Set' menu is a steal.

RANDALL & AUBIN

14–16 Brewer Street
Soho
London W1F 0SG
+44 2072874447
www.randallandaubin.com

Recommended by
Yotam Ottolenghi

Opening hours	Open 7 days
Credit cards	Accepted
Price range	Affordable
Style	Casual
Cuisine	French Seafood
Recommended for	Regular neighbourhood

'There is a great, buzzy Soho vibe; day or night it's always vibrant there. And the oysters are divine.'
—Yotam Ottolenghi

THE RED FORT

77 Dean Street
Soho
London W1D 3SH
+44 2074372525
www.redfort.co.uk

Recommended by
Dominic Chapman

Opening hours	Open 7 days
Credit cards	Accepted
Price range	Affordable
Style	Smart casual
Cuisine	Indian
Recommended for	Late night

'Probably the best curry in London. Brilliant chef and restaurant.'—Dominic Chapman

RONNIE SCOTT'S

47 Frith Street
Soho
London W1D 4HT
+44 2074390747
www.ronniescotts.co.uk

Recommended by
Chris Galvin

Opening hours	Open 7 days
Credit cards	Accepted
Price range	Affordable
Style	Smart casual
Cuisine	International
Recommended for	Late night

'I love jazz and this place makes for a great night out.'
—Chris Galvin

SOCIAL EATING HOUSE

58 Poland Street
Soho
London W1F 7NR
+44 2079933251
www.socialeatinghouse.com

Recommended by
Marcus Eaves

Opening hours	Closed Sunday
Credit cards	Accepted
Price range	Affordable
Style	Casual
Cuisine	Modern British
Recommended for	Local favourite

'New-wave "bistronomy". It's a slick operation with a chilled-out, funky vibe and stunning food.'
—Marcus Eaves

SOHO KITCHEN & BAR

Recommended by
Tom Aikens

19–21 Old Compton Street
Soho
London W1D 5JJ
+44 2077345656
www.sohokitchenandbar.co.uk

Opening hours	Open 7 days
Credit cards	Accepted
Price range	Affordable
Style	Casual
Cuisine	Bar-Diner
Recommended for	Late night

'Great location in Soho and they serve an all-day menu into the early hours with comfort-food favourites, plus a good selection of cocktails.'—Tom Aikens

SPUNTINO

Recommended by
Adam Byatt, Shaun
Hill, Karam Sethi

61 Rupert Street
Soho
London W1D 7PW
www.spuntino.co.uk

Opening hours	Open 7 days
Reservation policy	No
Credit cards	Accepted
Price range	Affordable
Style	Casual
Cuisine	Italian-American
Recommended for	Bargain

'I particularly like their core dishes – truffled egg and fontina on toast, the best sliders in London – and they have very reasonable house wines.'—Shaun Hill

Russell Norman's follow-up to Polpo channels the aesthetic of a hip Brooklyn diner meets a fashion-forward Lower Eastside speakeasy. It's darkly lit with artfully aged white tiles on the walls, rusty tin on the ceiling, alt-rock soundtrack and a U-shaped zinc-topped counter around which sit twenty-six fixed stools. No telephone, no reservations, and a long wait at peak times for the menu of Italian-American small plates that take in various sliders, meatballs and pizzette. The popcorn machine churns out complimentary cups of the salty snack laced with chilli to make you thirsty for the predominantly Italian and reasonably priced wine list.

TONKOTSU

Recommended by
Tom Oldroyd

63 Dean Street
Soho
London W1D 4QG
+44 2074370071
www.tonkotsu.co.uk

Opening hours	Open 7 days
Reservation policy	No
Credit cards	Accepted
Price range	Budget
Style	Casual
Cuisine	Ramen Noodles
Recommended for	Late night

'If I'm in need of something a little more substantial, then you'll find me at Tonkotsu's bar, my head simmering in a steaming bowl of slippery ramen broth.'—Tom Oldroyd

WRIGHT BROTHERS

Recommended by
Rainer Becker

13 Kingly Street
Soho
London W1B 5PW
+44 2074343611
www.thewrightbrothers.co.uk

Opening hours	Open 7 days
Credit cards	Accepted
Price range	Affordable
Style	Smart casual
Cuisine	Seafood
Recommended for	Regular neighbourhood

'Simple, good, honest food in a vibrant location – and great oysters!'—Rainer Becker

YAUATCHA

15–17 Broadwick Street
Soho
London W1F 0DL
+44 2074948888
www.yauatcha.com

Recommended by
Matthew Harris,
Mats Vollmer

Opening hours	Open 7 days
Credit cards	Accepted
Price range	Affordable
Style	Smart casual
Cuisine	Chinese
Recommended for	Worth the travel

'I had the big menu and the Peking duck I got as the last dish was perfect. Impressed!'—Mats Vollmer

CAFE MURANO

33 St James's Street
St James's
London SW1A 1HD
+44 2033715559
www.cafemurano.co.uk

Recommended by
Neil Borthwick

Opening hours	Closed Sunday
Credit cards	Accepted
Price range	Affordable
Style	Casual
Cuisine	Italian Bistro
Recommended for	Late night

'It's rare in London to find a place where you can get a stunning bowl of pasta and a glass of wine in an informal, buzzy room. Their post-theatre menu is fantastic value. Of course I love the grown-up big sister Murano too when I have more time to indulge.' —Neil Borthwick

SHORYU RAMEN

9 Regent Street
St James's
London SW1Y 4LR
www.shoryuramen.com

Recommended by
Atul Kochhar,
Yotam Ottolenghi

Opening hours	Open 7 days
Reservation policy	No
Credit cards	Accepted
Price range	Budget
Style	Casual
Cuisine	Ramen Noodles
Recommended for	Late night

'I love places that do one thing very well — you know you are in good hands. Noodles late at night hit the spot for me: comforting, easy, sustaining and quick.' —Yotam Ottolenghi

LONDON

EAST

$\hat{N}$

SCALE

0   400   800   1200
└─────┴─────┴─────┘ yd.

40 MALTBY STREET

Recommended by
James Lowe, Ed Wilson

40 Maltby Street
Bermondsey
London SE1 3PA
+44 2072379247
www.40maltbystreet.com

Opening hours	Closed Sunday to Tuesday
Reservation policy	No
Credit cards	Accepted but not AMEX
Price range	Affordable
Style	Casual
Cuisine	British
Recommended for	Regular neighbourhood

'The best daily-changing menu of simple seasonal food and a great wine list. You always leave happy and content with life.'—Ed Wilson

Locals weren't too pleased when this idiosyncratic venture in a rattling railway arch hit the headlines, but with its serious food and no-fuss presentation, it wasn't going to stay secret for long. Maltby Street was dubbed the 'next Borough Market', and while that hasn't really happened, it has spawned good ad-hoc eateries – not least this wine bar and shop with a handful of tables and limited service hours. There are unusual natural wines from France, Italy and Slovenia at goodish mark-ups, but it's the (mismatched) small plates – deep fried duck eggs, say, or glazed Yorkshire ham – which really take centre stage.

CAFE EAST

Recommended by
Sam Harris

100 Redriff Road
Bermondsey
London SE16 7LH
www.cafeeastpho.co.uk

Opening hours	Closed Tuesday
Reservation policy	No
Credit cards	Not accepted
Price range	Budget
Style	Casual
Cuisine	Vietnamese
Recommended for	Bargain

'The best pho soup in London, so authentic.'
—Sam Harris

CASSE-CROÛTE

Recommended by
Olivier Limousin

109 Bermondsey Street
Bermondsey
London SE1 3XB
+44 2074072140
www.cassecroute.co.uk

Opening hours	Open 7 days
Credit cards	Accepted
Price range	Affordable
Style	Casual
Cuisine	French Bistro
Recommended for	Local favourite

'Typical French bistro with everything reminding me of my country – the music, the food, the aperitifs…'
—Olivier Limousin

THE GARRISON

Recommended by
Tom Sellers

99–101 Bermondsey Street
Bermondsey
London SE1 3XB
+44 2070899355
www.thegarrison.co.uk

Opening hours	Open 7 days
Credit cards	Accepted
Price range	Affordable
Style	Casual
Cuisine	Gastro pub
Recommended for	Breakfast

'Nice variety on the menu so I can get whatever I am in the mood for.'—Tom Sellers

JOSÉ

Recommended by
Tom Sellers

104 Bermondsey Street
Bermondsey
London SE1 3UB
www.josepizarro.com/restaurants/jose

Opening hours	Open 7 days
Reservation policy	No
Credit cards	Accepted
Price range	Budget
Style	Casual
Cuisine	Tapas
Recommended for	Regular neighbourhood

'The food is great, the venue is small and intimate and the atmosphere is really friendly.'—Tom Sellers

ZUCCA

184 Bermondsey Street
Bermondsey
London SE1 3TQ
+44 2073786809
www.zuccalondon.com

Recommended by
Adam Byatt, Angela
Hartnett, Philip Howard,
José Pizarro, Clare Smyth

Opening hours	Closed Monday
Credit cards	Accepted but not AMEX
Price range	Affordable
Style	Casual
Cuisine	Italian
Recommended for	Regular neighbourhood

'A great local restaurant serving the kind of food I like to eat regularly.'—Philip Howard

Since opening in 2010 in fashionable Bermondsey Street, not far from the foodie hub of Borough Market, Zucca has become a fixture on the London food scene. Part of the new wave of affordable, rustic Italians in London, plain, excellently executed dishes such as grilled octopus, sprouting (baby) broccoli, rosemary and anchovy, and home-made pasta with lentils, walnuts and basil are served up in this plain but cheerful canteen-like space. The simple stylishness keeps prices down – all the better to enjoy the extensive, all-Italian wine list that saw Zucca win *Decanter* magazine's 'Restaurant of the Year' title in 2011.

BISTROTHEQUE

23–27 Wadeson Street
Bethnal Green
London E2 9DR
+44 2089837900
www.bistrotheque.com

Recommended by
Ben Tish

Opening hours	Open 7 days
Credit cards	Accepted
Price range	Affordable
Style	Casual
Cuisine	Bistro
Recommended for	Breakfast

'Apart from a first-class fry up when you need it most (on a hangover), there's always amazing entertainment in the form of a transvestite playing renditions of pop and club classics.'—Ben Tish

CIAO BELLA

86–90 Lamb's Conduit Street
Bloomsbury
London WC1N 3LZ
+44 2072424119
www.ciaobellarestaurant.co.uk

Recommended by
Fergus Henderson

Opening hours	Open 7 days
Credit cards	Accepted
Price range	Affordable
Style	Casual
Cuisine	Italian
Recommended for	Regular neighbourhood

'They tolerate kids, the best people-watching in Lamb's Conduit Street, you can sit outside comfortably to smoke, which suits some of us, and they leave the grappa on the table.'—Fergus Henderson

AQUA SHARD

The Shard
31F, 31 St Thomas Street
Borough
London SE1 9RY
+44 2030111256
www.aquashard.co.uk

Recommended by
Manoj Vasaikar

Opening hours	Open 7 days
Credit cards	Accepted
Price range	Expensive
Style	Smart casual
Cuisine	British
Recommended for	Late night

'Great atmosphere. London looks beautiful from up there. Great cocktails.'—Manoj Vasaikar

BRINDISA CHORIZO GRILL

Recommended by
Alfred Prasad

Borough Market
The Floral Hall
Stoney Street
Borough
London SE1 9AF
+44 2074071036
www.brindisa.com

Opening hours	Closed Sunday
Reservation policy	No
Credit cards	Accepted
Price range	Budget
Style	Casual
Cuisine	Spanish
Recommended for	Bargain

'Love their double chorizo sandwich – under £5 – with high-quality chorizo, just taken off a sizzling grill, sandwiched in a ciabatta with crisp rocket and juicy piquillo peppers. Just across the street is Monmouth Café for a perfect filter coffee. Meal done for under £7.'—Alfred Prasad

HUTONG

Recommended by
José Pizarro

The Shard
33F, 31 St Thomas Street
Borough
London SE1 9RY
+44 2030111257
www.aquahutong.co.uk

Opening hours	Open 7 days
Credit cards	Accepted
Price range	Expensive
Style	Smart casual
Cuisine	Chinese
Recommended for	Regular neighbourhood

'The food and the view are both amazing!'
—José Pizarro

MAGDALEN

Recommended by
Sam Harris

152 Tooley Street
Borough
London SE1 2TU
+44 2074031342
www.magdalenrestaurant.co.uk

Opening hours	Closed Sunday
Credit cards	Accepted
Price range	Affordable
Style	Smart casual
Cuisine	British
Recommended for	Regular neighbourhood

'This place seems to have been missed by Londoners – such is the shame, as the quality of cooking is some of the best in town. My meal is perfect every time, and I'm very fussy!'—Sam Harris

OBLIX

Recommended by
Giorgio Locatelli

The Shard
32F, 31 St Thomas Street
Borough
London SE1 9RY
+44 2072686700
www.oblixrestaurant.com

Opening hours	Open 7 days
Credit cards	Accepted
Price range	Expensive
Style	Smart casual
Cuisine	International
Recommended for	Local favourite

'The food is great and the view is breathtaking.'
—Giorgio Locatelli

FRANCO MANCA

Recommended by
Jonathan Jones, Mikael
Jonsson, Isaac McHale,
Shuko Oda

Unit 4, Market Row
Brixton
London SW9 8LD
+44 2077383021
www.francomanca.co.uk

Opening hours	Open 7 days
Reservation policy	No
Credit cards	Accepted but not AMEX
Price range	Budget
Style	Casual
Cuisine	Pizza
Recommended for	Bargain

'Every time I am stunned by how good it is, and how cheap the bill is at the end.'—Isaac McHale

HONEST BURGERS

Recommended by
Robin Gill

Unit 12, Brixton Village
Brixton
London SW9 8PR
+44 2077337963
www.honestburgers.co.uk

Opening hours	Open 7 days
Reservation policy	No
Credit cards	Accepted
Price range	Budget
Style	Casual
Cuisine	Burgers
Recommended for	Bargain

'Honest Burgers has simply the best burger in town. Always an interesting beer list too.'—Robin Gill

KAOSARN

Recommended by
Sami Tamimi

Unit 96, Brixton Village
Brixton
London SW9 8PR
+44 2070958922

Opening hours	Closed Monday
Credit cards	Not accepted
Price range	Budget
Style	Casual
Cuisine	Thai
Recommended for	Late night

'The atmosphere in Brixton market is great – you can eat in the market cheaply so there's always a really mixed and happy crowd there, tucking into lots of different things. Drinks in one place, burgers in another, coffee and cake right next door. There is something for everyone. And you can get the best marinated chicken with sticky rice and a green papaya salad south of the river if you're happy to join the queue outside KaoSarn.'—Sami Tamimi

SILK ROAD

Recommended by
Shuko Oda,
Junya Yamasaki

49 Camberwell Church Street
Camberwell
London SE5 8TR
+44 2077034832

Opening hours	Open 7 days
Credit cards	Not accepted
Price range	Budget
Style	Casual
Cuisine	Chinese
Recommended for	Bargain

'At least twice a month I get a craving for their spicy stir-fried cabbage and chewy belt noodles. Cheap and cheerful.'—Shuko Oda

Camberwell's no frills Silk Road specializes in the food of Xinjiang, China's northwest frontier province. The basic set-up of communal tables and punishingly hard benches isn't what brings London's gluttons back again and again: that would be the fascinating regional cuisine with its central Asian and Chinese influences and the great value it represents. Few leave without trying the fried pork dumplings, chilli and cumin lamb skewers and 'big plate' chicken in fiery broth, with its side of hand-pulled noodles for optimal slurping. A feast and a few Tsingtao beers still leave change from £20.

TASTE OF SIAM

Recommended by
Giorgio Locatelli

45 Camden High Street
Camden
London NW1 7JH
+44 2073800665
www.taste-of-siam.co.uk

Opening hours	Open 7 days
Credit cards	Accepted
Price range	Budget
Style	Casual
Cuisine	Thai
Recommended for	Bargain

'It's cheap and cheerful.'—Giorgio Locatelli

BARBECOA

20 New Change Passage
City of London
London EC4M 9AG
+44 2030058555
www.barbecoa.com

Opening hours	Open 7 days
Credit cards	Accepted
Price range	Affordable
Style	Casual
Cuisine	Barbeque
Recommended for	Wish I'd opened

'A very good concept, with its own butchery. The whole atmosphere is screaming "We have the best meat in town". Also, the design of the kitchen, with the big Argentinian grill in front of the window, is amazing.'
—Arjan Wennekes

DUCK & WAFFLE

Heron Tower
110 Bishopsgate
City of London
London EC2N 4AY
+44 2036407310
www.duckandwaffle.com

Opening hours	Open 7 days
Credit cards	Accepted
Price range	Affordable
Style	Smart casual
Cuisine	European
Recommended for	Breakfast

'Even if the food was half as good as it actually is, I'd still enjoy eating there purely because of the views. To get food that actually delivers in a restaurant that high up is a huge gain for London. Dan has a filthy mind when it comes to food and that is never better utilised than during breakfast/brunch, which for me is all about layering on the carbs, fats and sugars. I don't eat breakfast that often, but if I want healthy I'll buy some porridge and stay at home. If I'm going out then there is no better place.'—Neil Rankin

HAWKSMOOR

10 Basinghall Street
City of London
London EC2V 5BQ
+44 2073978120
www.thehawksmoor.com

Opening hours	Closed Saturday and Sunday
Credit cards	Accepted
Price range	Expensive
Style	Smart casual
Cuisine	Steakhouse
Recommended for	Breakfast

'The Hawksmoor breakfast is a beast of a feast and they have great cocktails too. Perfect cure after a heavy night.'—Robin Gill

The weekday breakfast menu offered only at this branch of Hawksmoor is worth a special trip to the City. Not least for the that's-what-I-call-a-power-breakfast excess of their eye-opening platter for two, which includes a smoked bacon chop; their own-recipe sausages made with pork, beef and mutton; black pudding; short-rib bubble and squeak; grilled bone marrow; 'Trotter baked beans'; fried eggs; grilled mushrooms; and roast tomatoes. Combine that with several Bloody Marys – you can pimp your own from a buffet of condiments should you wish – and you'll be set up for the day. Or possibly for a lie-down.

MOSHI MOSHI

Liverpool Street Station
Unit 24
City of London
London EC2M 7QH
+44 2072473227
www.moshimoshi.co.uk

Opening hours	Closed Saturday and Sunday
Credit cards	Accepted
Price range	Affordable
Style	Casual
0Cuisine	Sushi
Recommended for	Regular neighbourhood

'Caroline Bennett's team serve excellent, fresh, sustainably caught Cornish fish. I like to be able to trust restaurants, and here I can.'—Peter Weeden

SWEETINGS

39 Queen Victoria Street
City of London
London EC4N 4SF
+44 2072483062

Recommended by
Fergus Henderson,
Jacob Kenedy

Opening hours............................Closed Saturday and Sunday
Reservation policy...No
Credit cards...Accepted
Price range...Affordable
Style...Casual
Cuisine...Seafood
Recommended for...Local favourite

'It's been around for about 200 years and is perfectly unfussy, unspoilt, in-your-face London with friendly service and brilliant seafood.'—Jacob Kenedy

Serving simply prepared fish in the City of London since 1889, without being pompous Sweetings revels in being fantastically old fashioned, a right earned by having survived two world wars and more financial crashes than you can a shake a skate wing at. It's the like of crab bisque, smoked eel, potted shrimps, fried whitebait and scallops and bacon to start, with main courses running from extravagant, simply prepared catches such as turbot and Dover sole, to their infinitely more affordable fish pie and salmon cake. Puddings are hefty boarding-school classics such as baked jam roll and spotted dick.

CARAVAN

11–13 Exmouth Market
Clerkenwell
London EC1R 4QD
+44 2078338115
www.caravanonexmouth.co.uk

Recommended by
Brad Farmerie

Opening hours...Open 7 days
Credit cards...Accepted
Price range...Affordable
Style...Casual
Cuisine...Modern International
Recommended for...Breakfast

'Maybe the best coffee you have ever had, with delicious food and casual, cool service.'
—Brad Farmerie

Caravan sits at the mouth of Exmouth Market, where creatives and crusties rub shoulders with Post Office workers. The all-day menu, a well-travelled selection of snacks, small plates and grown-up main courses, is no slouch. But it's perhaps for breakfast or a relaxed weekend brunch, sat over their take on the classic fry-up or a plate of baked eggs with chorizo, that its charms are best appreciated. They roast their own coffee beans in the basement: the combination of aroma, choice – from Flat Whites to proper filter – and quality are more than enough to satisfy even the most discerning of coffee geeks.

THE MODERN PANTRY

47–48 St John's Square
Clerkenwell
London EC1V 4JJ
+44 2075539210
www.themodernpantry.co.uk

Recommended by
Pascal Aussignac, Ollie
Dabbous, Angela Hartnett

Opening hours	Open 7 days
Credit cards	Accepted
Price range	Affordable
Style	Casual
Cuisine	Modern International
Recommended for	Breakfast

'I love Anna Hansen's cuisine and her approach to British ingredients with a fusion twist.'
—Pascal Aussignac

The Modern Pantry's bright ground-floor café, with its all-white tables and chairs that amplify the light through its large front windows across St John's Square, is the perfect morning venue. Raised in New Zealand, chef-proprietor Anna Hansen puts as much care into breakfast as she does lunch and dinner. Expect the likes of ricotta pancakes, soft-boiled eggs with Vegemite soldiers and grilled chorizo with plantain fritters. Star of the show is a, rightly celebrated, Sri Lankan-inspired omelette filled with sugar-cured prawns, green chilli, spring onions and coriander, topped with a smoked chilli sambal. The smoothies also demand your attention.

MORITO

32 Exmouth Market
Clerkenwell
London EC1R 4QE
+44 2072787007
www.morito.co.uk

Recommended by
Yotam Ottolenghi

Opening hours	Open 7 days
Credit cards	Accepted
Price range	Affordable
Style	Casual
Cuisine	Tapas
Recommended for	Regular neighbourhood

'The atmosphere is great, the crowd is mixed, the tapas is first class. Stopping by for a snack and a drink on Exmouth Market always reminds me why I love living and working in London. And I could eat a bucket of the beetroot borani with feta, dill, walnuts and nigella seeds.'—Yotam Ottolenghi

MORO

34–36 Exmouth Market
Clerkenwell
London EC1R 4QE
+44 2078338336
www.moro.co.uk

Recommended by
Angela Hartnett, Jacob
Kenedy, Miles Kirby, Tom
Pemberton, Tim Siadatan,
Michael Smith

Opening hours	Open 7 days
Credit cards	Accepted
Price range	Affordable
Style	Casual
Cuisine	North African-Spanish
Recommended for	Regular neighbourhood

'Diverse, cosmopolitan, interesting, busy, fun, exciting and unique – just like London.'—Tom Siadatan

OTTO'S

182 Gray's Inn Road
Clerkenwell
London WC1X 8EW
+44 2077130107
www.ottos-restaurant.com

Recommended by
Jonathan Jones

Opening hours	Closed Sunday
Credit cards	Accepted
Price range	Expensive
Style	Casual
Cuisine	French
Recommended for	High end

'Pressed duck over two courses and very well-priced Burgundy. It is a labour of love for the incredibly hospitable Otto.'—Jonathan Jones

THE QUALITY CHOP HOUSE

88–94 Farringdon Road
Clerkenwell
London EC1R 3EA
+44 2072781452
www.thequalitychophouse.com

Recommended by
Isaac McHale, Neil
Rankin, Peter Weeden,
Ed Wilson

Opening hours	Open 7 days
Credit cards	Accepted
Price range	Affordable
Style	Casual
Cuisine	British
Recommended for	Local favourite

'Like the rest of London, The Quality Chop House has a rich past, but has been reinvented and reinvigorated by some clever people to make it what it is today. Go.'
—Isaac McHale

SUSHI TETSU

12 Jerusalem Passage
Clerkenwell
London EC1V 4JP
+44 2032170090
www.sushitetsu.co.uk

Recommended by
James Knappett,
Nuno Mendes

Opening hours	Closed Monday and Sunday
Credit cards	Accepted
Price range	Expensive
Style	Smart casual
Cuisine	Sushi
Recommended for	High end

'A wonderful sushi experience that is very personal and very special. It's almost as though the fish swims from the counter into your mouth – it's that fresh! The chef and his wife are the perfect hosts and make you feel totally at home sitting at the small eight-seat counter.'
—Nuno Mendes

MANGAL OCAKBASI

10 Arcola Street
Dalston
London E8 2DJ
+44 2072758981
www.mangal1.com

Recommended by
Nuno Mendes,
Yotam Ottolenghi

Opening hours	Open 7 days
Reservation policy	No
Credit cards	Not accepted
Price range	Budget
Style	Casual
Cuisine	Turkish
Recommended for	Bargain

'The no-frills focus on the kebabs, the kebabs! I always have the adana kofte with yogurt, tomato and butter sauce.'—Yotam Ottolenghi

SÖMINE

131 Kingsland High Street
Dalston
London E8 2PB
+44 2072547384

Recommended by
Samantha & Samuel Clark

Opening hours	Open 7 days
Reservation policy	No
Credit cards	Accepted
Price range	Budget
Style	Casual
Cuisine	Turkish
Recommended for	Late night

'A twenty-four-hour Turkish restaurant on the corner of Kingsland Road and Crossway. We go there for Turkish mezze, yogurt soups and delicious slow-cooked dishes. The Turkish restaurants around Dalston and Stoke Newington were a great influence on Moro, before and when we first opened. There are many and it is hard to have a bad meal if you stick to the basics: marinated lamb kofte or shish kebab, quail or chicken, grilled over charcoal with the freshest of chopped salads, yogurt and bread. The perfect late-night sustenance and Sömine happens to be open late; in fact it never closes!'—Samantha & Samuel Clark

TAVA RESTAURANT

17 Stoke Newington Road
Dalston
London N16 8BH
+44 2072493666

Recommended by
Isaac McHale

Opening hours	Open 7 days
Credit cards	Accepted
Price range	Budget
Style	Casual
Cuisine	Turkish
Recommended for	Late night

'London doesn't really do much late-night stuff, considering its size. This is always my pick of late-night eats after work, great *lahmacun*.'—Isaac McHale

UMUT 2000

6 Crossway
Dalston
London N16 8HX
+44 2072490903
www.umut2000.com

Recommended by
Tom Harris, Ed Wilson

Opening hours	Open 7 days
Credit cards	Not accepted
Price range	Budget
Style	Casual
Cuisine	Turkish
Recommended for	Late night

'Smoky grilled lamb, the best sumac and onions, great breads and endless ice-cold bottles of Efes beer. There are lots of great Turkish restaurants in East London but Umut 2000 is always where I head to after a night out.' —Tom Harris

THE SIRLOIN

94 Cowcross Street
Farringdon
London EC1M 6BH
+44 2072501442

Recommended by
Fergus Henderson

Opening hours	Open 7 days
Credit cards	Accepted but not AMEX
Price range	Affordable
Style	Casual
Cuisine	Gastropub
Recommended for	Breakfast

'Offers a steadying fry up and pint of Guinness early in the morning. Strangely, every time I've been it's just me in the dining room, adding calmness to the start of the day.' —Fergus Henderson

This dining room can be found above the Farringdon boozer, The Hope, giving the whole the nickname The Hope & Sir Loin. On the doorstep of Smithfield meat market, it used to open stupidly early to serve meaty breakfasts to traders – those that humped carcasses for a living and drank pints, and those of the financial variety that guzzled Champagne. These days The Hope doesn't open its doors until a civilized 7.00 a.m. and only serves breakfast upstairs to large parties that book ahead. But their Full English – egg, sausage, bacon, liver, kidney and a sirloin steak – is still served in the ground-floor bar.

ST. JOHN BAR AND RESTAURANT

26 St John Street
Farringdon
London EC1M 4AY
+44 2072510848
www.stjohnrestaurant.com

Recommended by
Andreas Dahlberg,
Semsa Denizsel, Sam
Harris, Tom Harris, Margot
Henderson, Jonathan Jones,
Miles Kirby, Jeremy Lee,
Jp McMahon, Carlo Mirarchi,
Tom Oldroyd, Tom Pemberton,
Ruth Rogers, Shaun Searley,
Tom Sellers, Peter Weeden,
Junya Yamasaki

Opening hours	Open 7 days
Credit cards	Accepted
Price range	Affordable
Style	Casual
Cuisine	British
Recommended for	Local favourite

'This place represents the true side of London, not the over-hyped glamour of some of the Mayfair establishments. It marries the balance of an old working-class establishment with a cutting-edge, up-to-date one. It's one of a kind, and only a city like London could have a restaurant like this.' —Sam Harris

Arguably the most seminal London restaurant of the last twenty years, the original branch of St. John has barely changed since it opened back in 1994. The birthplace of Fergus Henderson's famed 'nose-to-tail' philosophy, the twice-daily-changing menu is still tersely written, strictly seasonal and still likes to make use of bits of beast that Anglo-Saxon chefs used to throw away, until he made them fashionable. The other star is the Georgian building, an old smokehouse, its high ceilings, whitewashed walls and surfeit of natural light somehow managing to make it feel like nowhere else in London, and somewhere that couldn't exist anywhere else.

BERNERS TAVERN

Recommended by
Ben Tish

10 Berners Street
Fitzrovia
London W1T 3NP
+44 2079087979
www.bernerstavern.com

Opening hours	Open 7 days
Credit cards	Accepted
Price range	Affordable
Style	Smart casual
Cuisine	British
Recommended for	Wish I'd opened

'It has to be the most beautiful dining room I've been in – anywhere – and Ian Schrager designed it. The food is fantastic too. It's rammed to the rafters for breakfast, lunch, afternoon tea and dinner seven days a week.' —Ben Tish

Jason Atherton's glamorous new all-day dining venture capped a remarkable 2013 for the chef, who also found time to launch Soho's Little Social and the Social Eating House. Naturally enough, given its setting in Ian Schrager's £33m Edition Hotel, it's a jaw-dropping space, with Grand Central Station-style chandeliers, walls packed with paintings, and an impressive backlit bar. With Atherton's long-time lieutenant Phil Carmichael heading up the kitchen, the inventive modern British cooking is just as stellar, balancing witty modernist touches reminiscent of his first venture, Pollen Street Social, with barbecued pulled pork sandwiches and crowd-pleasing roasts.

BUBBLEDOGS

Recommended by
Paul Foster, Matthew
Gaudet, Mette Hvarre
Gassner, Nuno Mendes,
Josh Murphy

70 Charlotte Street
Fitzrovia
London W1T 4QG
+44 2076377770
www.bubbledogs.co.uk

Opening hours	Closed Monday and Sunday
Credit cards	Accepted
Price range	Affordable
Style	Casual
Cuisine	Hot Dogs
Recommended for	Wish I'd opened

'Fast food and grower Champagne. It seems like a no-brainer now that I think about it.' —Josh Murphy

Run by an ex-Noma duo, this Champagne-and-hot-dog joint opened in 2012, and immediately won over both the hip and the jaded. Its concept is clever: single-estate Champagnes served not with caviar, as you'd expect, but gourmet dogs – from the Naked dog (a dog in a bun), to jazzed-up versions like the Trishna (topped with mango chutney and mint sauce). Sides include potato Tots and fresh coleslaw. The space itself is handsome, with exposed brick, reclaimed oak floorboards and a copper-clad bar – although the unisex toilets aren't for everyone. The owners' small-plate venture, Kitchen Table, is also on the premises.

DABBOUS

Recommended by
Tom Pemberton,
Thrainn Freyr Vigfússon

39 Whitfield Street
Fitzrovia
London W1T 2SF
+44 2073231544
www.dabbous.co.uk

Opening hours	Closed Monday and Sunday
Credit cards	Accepted
Price range	Affordable
Style	Casual
Cuisine	Modern European
Recommended for	Wish I'd opened

'Simple but beautiful presentation. Quality food in a trendy atmosphere.'—Tom Pemberton

Critics' darling on opening in 2012 meant Dabbous's compact thirty-six-cover dining room found itself booked until kingdom come. Believe the hype – the universal praise for the playful French-meets-Nordic-in-London cooking of its well-travelled young chef Ollie Dabbous (ex of Texture and Le Manoir) is more than justified. The gritty, no-frills, industrial aesthetic of the dining room – artfully distressed concrete, meshed metal, exposed ducting – has its detractors. But perhaps it's partially why everything – particularly the set lunch and the tasting menus – seems so reasonably priced and so much fun. The basement bar does classy cocktails and a short menu of bar snacks.

HONEY & CO.

Recommended by
Yotam Ottolenghi,
Sami Tamimi

25a Warren Street
Fitzrovia
London W1T 5LZ
+44 2073886175
www.honeyandco.co.uk

Opening hours	Closed Sunday
Credit cards	Accepted
Price range	Affordable
Style	Casual
Cuisine	Middle Eastern
Recommended for	Wish I'd opened

'It's hard to get a restaurant up and running and consistently in demand in London. Honey & Co. is a small, exceptionally good restaurant which has done just this. I don't wish I'd opened it – it's in the best hands – but I do wish I'd created their deconstructed cheesecake with a *kadaifi* pastry base. And they won't disclose the recipe!'—Yotam Ottolenghi

KITCHEN TABLE

Recommended by
Paul Foster, Adam Reid,
Shaun Searley

70 Charlotte Street
Fitzrovia
London W1T 4QG
+44 2076377770
www.kitchentablelondon.co.uk

Opening hours	Closed Monday and Sunday
Credit cards	Accepted
Price range	Expensive
Style	Smart casual
Cuisine	Modern European
Recommended for	Wish I'd opened

'The interaction the chefs have with the customers is great. There is a rawness and complete transparency to the restaurant as you literally sit around James Knappett's kitchen and watch him prepare your food. The best dining experience topped off with some of the best food being cooked right now.'—Shaun Searley

PIED À TERRE

Recommended by
Tom Pemberton

34 Charlotte Street
Fitzrovia
London W1T 2NH
+44 2076361178
www.pied-a-terre.co.uk

Opening hours	Closed Sunday
Credit cards	Accepted
Price range	Expensive
Style	Smart casual
Cuisine	Modern French
Recommended for	High end

'Consistent, excellent, with a lightness of touch.'
—Tom Pemberton

RIDING HOUSE CAFÉ

43–51 Great Titchfield Street
Fitzrovia
London W1W 7PQ
+44 2079270840
www.ridinghousecafe.co.uk

Opening hours	Open 7 days
Credit cards	Accepted
Price range	Affordable
Style	Casual
Cuisine	British bistro
Recommended for	Breakfast

'Not many places get breakfast right. They do.'
—Rainer Becker

ROKA

37 Charlotte Street
Fitzrovia
London W1T 1RR
+44 2075806464
www.rokarestaurant.com

Opening hours	Open 7 days
Credit cards	Accepted
Price range	Expensive
Style	Smart casual
Cuisine	Modern Japanese
Recommended for	High end

'I usually go for anything on the robata menu,
especially the lamb cutlets with Korean spices.'
—Karam Sethi

LARDO

197–201 Richmond Road
Hackney
London E8 3NJ
+44 2089852683
www.lardo.co.uk

Opening hours	Open 7 days
Credit cards	Accepted but not AMEX
Price range	Affordable
Style	Casual
Cuisine	Italian
Recommended for	Regular neighbourhood

'My kids go crazy for the pizzas, and they're amazing,
Damien is a great cook. But for me, it's date night,
sitting with my wife at the pass, drinking a Negroni
Sbagliato and sharing fennel-pollen salami and a bit
of lardy loin.'—Tom Harris

LUCKY CHIP

Netil Market Trailer
11–25 Westgate Street
Hackney
London E2 9AG
www.luckychipuk.com

Opening hours	Variable
Reservation policy	No
Credit cards	Accepted
Price range	Budget
Style	Casual
Cuisine	Burgers
Recommended for	Bargain

'The Kevin Bacon eaten outdoors is the best burger in
London.'—Ed Wilson

PALM2

Recommended by
Miles Kirby

152–156 Lower Clapton Road
Hackney
London E5 0QJ
+44 2085331787
www.palm2.co.uk

Opening hours	Open 7 days
Credit cards	Accepted
Price range	Budget
Style	Casual
Cuisine	International
Recommended for	Local favourite

'This place represents all walks of life in the borough of Hackney. Interesting produce and great *gözleme* (savoury Turkish pastry) to go. The pop-up space upstairs hosts some great nights too.'—Miles Kirby

In the fashionable East London frontier that Clapton has become, this hip grocers-cum-event space is a community hub in rapidly gentrifying E5. The shop punts everything from E5 Bakehouse bread to interesting wines and craft beers; it has a deli counter that does cheese, meat and fish, and a good selection of quality fruit and veg. Their upstairs event space hosts everything from the acquired taste that is Ukulele Wednesdays, to more obviously delicious residencies that are pizza pop-ups, sushi master classes, sake tastings, Ghanaian and Nepalese evenings, dim sum lunches and weekend brunches. Every food- and drink-geek's dream local.

PAVILION

Recommended by
Stevie Parle, Shaun Searley,
Steve Williams

Victoria Park
Crown Gate West
Hackney
London E9 7DE
+44 2089800030
www.the-pavilion-cafe.com

Opening hours	Open 7 days
Reservation policy	No
Credit cards	Accepted
Price range	Budget
Style	Casual
Cuisine	Café
Recommended for	Breakfast

'Situated in Victoria Park next to a lake, they focus on quality, locally sourced produce. No frills, simply food perfectly executed – just what you want for breakfast. And the coffee is always spot on.'—Shaun Searley

RAW DUCK

Recommended by
Nuno Mendes

197 Richmond Road
Hackney
London E8 3NJ
+44 2089866534
www.rawduckhackney.co.uk

Opening hours	Open 7 days
Credit cards	Accepted but not AMEX
Price range	Budget
Style	Casual
Cuisine	Café-Bistro
Recommended for	Regular neighbourhood

'It's a little place in Hackney that is open all day. They have a great natural wine list and a really interesting small menu that changes throughout the day. '—Nuno Mendes

VIOLET

Recommended by
Henry Harris

47 Wilton Way
Hackney
London E8 3ED
+44 2072758360
www.violetcakes.com

Opening hours	Closed Monday
Reservation policy	No
Credit cards	Accepted
Price range	Budget
Style	Casual
Cuisine	Bakery
Recommended for	Breakfast

'Superlative baking and properly made coffee.'—Henry Harris

THE WINDSOR CASTLE

Recommended by
Miles Kirby

135 Lower Clapton Road
Hackney
London E5 8EQ
+44 2089856096
www.thewindsorcastleclapton.com

Opening hours	Open 7 days
Credit cards	Accepted
Price range	Affordable
Style	Casual
Cuisine	British bistro
Recommended for	Regular neighbourhood

'Great pub with excellent food.'—Miles Kirby

BEAGLE

Recommended by
Nuno Mendes

397–400 Geffrye Street
Hoxton
London E2 8HZ
+44 2076132967
www.beaglelondon.co.uk

Opening hours	Open 7 days
Credit cards	Accepted
Price range	Affordable
Style	Casual
Cuisine	British bistro
Recommended for	Breakfast

'The brunch menu here is amazing. The whole
breakfast menu is super decadent and super tasty.
Last time I was there I had the portobello mushrooms,
toasted brioche, poached eggs and hollandaise.
They also do a great blood cake and hash browns.'
—Nuno Mendes

BRAWN

Recommended by
Angela Hartnett,
Margot Henderson

49 Columbia Road
Hoxton
London E2 7RG
+44 2077295692
www.brawn.co

Opening hours	Open 7 days
Credit cards	Accepted but not AMEX
Price range	Affordable
Style	Casual
Cuisine	Bar-Bistro
Recommended for	Regular neighbourhood

'Brilliant food.'—Angela Hartnett

The likeable follow-up to Terroirs, Brawn sits on
Columbia Road, in the hip heart of the East End.
Utilitarian furniture meets whitewashed walls, Pop
art, amusingly random bric-a-brac and a soundtrack
that's big on reggae. It's staffed by a mixture of pretty
young things and arty bearded blokes. The gutsy,
daily-changing menu, made for sharing, is divided
into five fairly self-explanatory sections: 'Taste
Ticklers', 'Pig', 'Larder', 'Stove' and 'Pudding'. All of
which is designed to go with a wine list that's big on
natural wines – or 'cloudy reds and murky whites'
as they like to describe them.

THE BREAKFAST CLUB

Recommended by
Pascal Aussignac

2–4 Rufus Street
Hoxton
London N1 6PE
+44 2077295252
www.thebreakfastclubcafes.com

Opening hours	Open 7 days
Credit cards	Accepted
Price range	Budget
Style	Casual
Cuisine	Diner-Café
Recommended for	Breakfast

'Great diversity of food, atmosphere, smiley service,
cool 1980s music.'—Pascal Aussignac

EMBASSY EAST

Recommended by
Ed Wilson

285 Hoxton Street
Hoxton
London N1 5JX
+44 2077398340
www.embassyeast.co.uk

Opening hours	Open 7 days
Credit cards	Accepted but not AMEX
Price range	Budget
Style	Casual
Cuisine	Café
Recommended for	Breakfast

'The best grilled cheese sandwiches and coffee, by a great bunch of New Zealanders.'—Ed Wilson

SÔNG QUÊ CAFÉ

Recommended by
Greg Marchand

134 Kingsland Road
Hoxton
London E2 8DY
+44 2076133222
www.songque.co.uk

Opening hours	Open 7 days
Credit cards	Accepted but not AMEX or Diners
Price range	Budget
Style	Casual
Cuisine	Vietnamese
Recommended for	Bargain

'A great Vietnamese place full of Vietnamese and locals. They serve a killer quail.'—Greg Marchand

THE TOWPATH CAFÉ

Recommended by
Samantha & Samuel
Clark, Miles Kirby

42 De Beauvoir Crescent
Hoxton
London N1 5SB

Opening hours	Closed Monday
Reservation policy	No
Credit cards	Accepted
Price range	Budget
Style	Casual
Cuisine	Café
Recommended for	Local favourite

'An idyllic spot beside Regent's Canal in East London. The Towpath is a pretty hard location to beat, especially as it is combined with some of the most delicious food. Not surprisingly it is very popular.'
—Samantha & Samuel Clark

AFGHAN KITCHEN

Recommended by
Miles Kirby

35 Islington Green
Islington
London N1 8DU
+44 2073598019

Opening hours	Closed Monday and Sunday
Credit cards	Not accepted
Price range	Budget
Style	Casual
Cuisine	Afghan
Recommended for	Bargain

'The chicken and yogurt at the Afghan Kitchen is a bargain.'—Miles Kirby

ANTEPLILER

Recommended by
Jacob Kenedy, Ben Tish

139 Upper Street
Islington
London N1 1QP
+44 2072265441
www.anteplilerislington.co.uk

Opening hours	Open 7 days
Credit cards	Accepted but not AMEX or Diners
Price range	Budget
Style	Casual
Cuisine	Turkish
Recommended for	Bargain

'London is blessed with any number of Turkish restaurants – this is by far the best, and at bargain prices. They make brilliant baklava, too, for after the pide, mezze and grills.'—Jacob Kenedy

This welcoming Turkish restaurant is a rather different beast to its Green Lanes sister – all neon mosaics and Ottoman chic, in lieu of a functional canteen and patisserie – but has thankfully remained immune to the prices of its gentrified Islington neighbours. The food remains just as honest as before, too, with superior standards such as hummus, borek and kebabs, alongside Antep kitchen specials, originating from the Gaziantep province, near the Syrian border. Of particular wallet-friendly note are the wood-fired-oven *lahmacun*: thin Turkish pizzas topped with lamb, herbs and salad, and rolled up to create the most extraordinary comfort food.

LE COQ

Recommended by
Tim Siadatan

292–294 St Paul's Road
Islington
London N1 2LH
+44 2073595055
www.le-coq.co.uk

Opening hours	Closed Monday
Credit cards	Accepted
Price range	Affordable
Style	Casual
Cuisine	Rotisserie
Recommended for	Late night

'You can go at 10:30 p.m. and get the best rotisserie chicken in London, in under five minutes.'
—Tim Siadatan

DELHI GRILL

Recommended by
Ben Tish

21 Chapel Market
Islington
London N1 9EZ
+44 2072788100
www.delhigrill.com

Opening hours	Open 7 days
Credit cards	Accepted
Price range	Budget
Style	Casual
Cuisine	Indian
Recommended for	Bargain

'Delhi Grill serves delicious, fresh and interesting Indian tandoor grills, home-made breads and chutneys, and healthy, spicy salads. Always under £20 per head – even with a beer.'—Ben Tish

THE DUKE OF CAMBRIDGE

Recommended by
Francesco Mazzei

30 St Peter's Street
Islington
London N1 8JT
+44 2073593066
www.dukeorganic.co.uk

Opening hours	Open 7 days
Credit cards	Accepted
Price range	Affordable
Style	Casual
Cuisine	Gastropub
Recommended for	Local favourite

MAISON D'ÊTRE

Recommended by
Tim Siadatan

154 Canonbury Road
Islington
London N1 2UP
www.maisondetrecafe.co.uk

Opening hours	Open 7 days
Reservation policy	No
Credit cards	Accepted
Price range	Budget
Style	Casual
Cuisine	Café-Bistro
Recommended for	Breakfast

'Nice staff, great coffee and superb granola.'
—Tim Siadatan

OTTOLENGHI

Recommended by
Fisun Ercan,
Anna Hansen

287 Upper Street
Islington
London N1 2TZ
+44 2072881454
www.ottolenghi.co.uk

Opening hours	Open 7 days
Credit cards	Accepted
Price range	Affordable
Style	Casual
Cuisine	Modern International
Recommended for	Local favourite

'Eclectic menus. Fresh, vibrant food served all day, every day. Their use of global ingredients reflects modern living in London.'—Anna Hansen

PALMERA OASIS

Recommended by
Miles Kirby

332 Essex Road
Islington
London N1 3PB
+44 2077046149
www.palmeraoasis.co.uk

Opening hours	Open 7 days
Credit cards	Accepted but not AMEX or Diners
Price range	Budget
Style	Casual
Cuisine	Lebanese
Recommended for	Late night

'Extra tahini sauce.'—Miles Kirby

SMOKEHOUSE
63–69 Canonbury Road
Islington
London N1 2DG
+44 2073541144
www.smokehouseislington.co.uk

Recommended by
Paul Day, Shaun Searley

Opening hours	Open 7 days
Credit cards	Accepted
Price range	Affordable
Style	Casual
Cuisine	Gastropub
Recommended for	Regular neighbourhood

'I love their use of the Big Green Egg ceramic barbeque as I use it myself and I enjoy sampling all the creative ways it can be used. The food at Smokehouse is great and is accompanied by an extensive beer list.'
—Shaun Searley

SUNDAY
169 Hemingford Road
Islington
London N1 1DA
+44 2076073868

Recommended by
Anna Hansen

Opening hours	Open 7 days
Credit cards	Accepted
Price range	Affordable
Style	Casual
Cuisine	Café
Recommended for	Breakfast

'Fantastic brunches in a cute, friendly neighbourhood restaurant. It has a lovely garden out the back with a huge old fig tree, which is perfect in the summer. The food is generous, consistent and tasty.'—Anna Hansen

TRULLO
300–302 St Paul's Road
Islington
London N1 2LH
+44 2072262733
www.trullorestaurant.com

Recommended by
Miles Kirby

Opening hours	Open 7 days
Credit cards	Accepted but not AMEX or Diners
Price range	Affordable
Style	Casual
Cuisine	Italian
Recommended for	Regular neighbourhood

CARAVAN
Granary Building
1 Granary Square
King's Cross
London N1C 4AA
+44 2071017661
www.caravankingscross.co.uk

Recommended by
Giorgio Locatelli

Opening hours	Open 7 days
Credit cards	Accepted
Price range	Affordable
Style	Casual
Cuisine	Modern International
Recommended for	Wish I'd opened

'It does pizza, small eats and it's a fun but relaxing environment.'—Giorgio Locatelli

THE BEGGING BOWL
168 Bellenden Road
Peckham
London SE15 4BW
+44 2076352627
www.thebeggingbowl.co.uk

Recommended by
Matthew Harris

Opening hours	Open 7 days
Reservation policy	No
Credit cards	Accepted
Price range	Affordable
Style	Casual
Cuisine	Thai small plates
Recommended for	Worth the travel

'Fantastic, fresh, authentic.'—Matthew Harris

It's tempting to describe The Begging Bowl as an instant success, but this is merely the latest stop on chef Andy Oliver's personal Thai-food odyssey, which has involved six months in Bangkok restaurant Bo. Lan, a sous position at Alan Yau's Naamyaa, and... oh, the slight distraction of being a MasterChef finalist in 2009. All this experience and relentless enthusiasm is on display in this bright and informal Peckham restaurant, where colourful regional Thai dishes are made with the best British ingredients — think vermicelli noodles with Dorset crab, or Woodvale venison with chilli jam. Customers are treated like old friends, and prices are never unreasonable.

ALBION CAFE

Recommended by
Sam Harris

2–4 Boundary Street
Shoreditch
London E2 7DD
+44 2077291051
www.albioncaff.co.uk

Opening hours	Open 7 days
Reservation policy	No
Credit cards	Accepted
Price range	Affordable
Style	Casual
Cuisine	British
Recommended for	Breakfast

'The home-made breads are worth the trip alone, as are their pastries.'—Sam Harris

BEIGEL BAKE

Recommended by
Robin Gill, Tom Harris

159 Brick Lane
Shoreditch
London E1 6SB
+44 2077290616

Opening hours	Open 7 days
Reservation policy	No
Credit cards	Not accepted
Price range	Budget
Style	Casual
Cuisine	Bakery
Recommended for	Local favourite

'Bagels are part of my DNA. I've been going there since I was a kid and the first night I could legally drive, I drove all the way from Shepherd's Bush to Brick Lane to buy a salt beef and mustard bagel to celebrate. It was 3.00 a.m. and well worth the trip. I used to take girls there on dates and when I got married, the bagels at my wedding weren't going to come from anywhere else.'—Tom Harris

BURRO E SALVIA

Recommended by
Martin Morales

52 Redchurch Street
Shoreditch
London E2 7DP
+44 2077394429
www.burroesalvia.co.uk

Opening hours	Open 7 days
Credit cards	Accepted but not AMEX
Price range	Affordable
Style	Casual
Cuisine	Italian Deli-Café
Recommended for	Regular neighbourhood

'There is an incredibly high level of human craftsmanship in what they offer. It's a small pasta specialist where the focus is on real, artisanal Italian food similar in ethos to our very own values.'—Martin Morales

THE CLOVE CLUB

Recommended by
Tom Adams, Massimo
Bottura, Ben Greeno, Anna
Hansen, Tom Harris, James
Lowe, Brad McDonald, Stevie
Parle, Neil Rankin, René
Redzepi, Ed Wilson

Shoreditch Town Hall
380 Old Street
Shoreditch
London EC1V 9LT
+44 2077296496
www.thecloveclub.com

Opening hours	Closed Sunday
Credit cards	Accepted
Price range	Expensive
Style	Smart casual
Cuisine	Modern British
Recommended for	Wish I'd opened

'What a great cuisine guys! At a more than reasonable price in the centre of London, you find an authentically British menu with a contemporary touch. The restaurant is well maintained and elegant in the rooms of the old town hall. At the bar, quality drinks with character are prepared and the competence and courtesy of the staff is really top class.'—Massimo Bottura

Cult Dalston pop-up, The Clove Club found a permanent home in a section of Shoreditch Town Hall, opening in March 2013. The space is split between bar and dinner-only dining room. The latter, a handsome combination of lofty ceiling and open kitchen with show pass, serves a take-it-or-leave-it five-course menu with a few snacks thrown in for fun. The cooking combines carefully sourced British produce, a Nordic sensibility and more far-flung influences – notably a fondness for Korean condiments. Lunch, served in the bar, offers a more pared-back menu but the full tasting can be booked ahead of time.

DISHOOM SHOREDITCH

7 Boundary Street
Shoreditch
London E2 7JE
+44 2074209324
www.dishoom.com

Recommended by
Anna Hansen,
Stevie Parle,
Sami Tallberg

Opening hours...Open 7 days
Credit cards..Accepted
Price range...Affordable
Style...Casual
Cuisine...Indian
Recommended for..................................Late night

'Great atmosphere and a really fun restaurant.'
—Stevie Parle

FIFTEEN

15 Westland Place
Shoreditch
London N1 7LP
+44 2033751515
www.fifteen.net

Recommended by
Michael Toscano

Opening hours...Open 7 days
Credit cards..Accepted
Price range...Affordable
Style...Casual
Cuisine..European
Recommended for........................Wish I'd opened

'At Fifteen, Jamie Oliver has set up an apprenticeship
programme to give unemployed young people a job
and a chance to have a better life through learning
how to cook. I admire Jamie Oliver for all of his
philanthropic efforts.'—Michael Toscano

HOI POLLOI

Ace Hotel
100 Shoreditch High Street
Shoreditch
London E1 6JQ
+44 2088806100
www.hoi-polloi.co.uk

Recommended by
Isaac McHale

Opening hours...Open 7 days
Credit cards..Accepted
Price range...Affordable
Style...Smart casual
Cuisine..............................Modern British
Recommended for..............................Breakfast

'I love the glamorous room and buzzy atmosphere.'
—Isaac McHale

KÊU BÁNH MÌ DELI

332 Old Street
Shoreditch
London EC1V 9DR
+44 2077391164
www.keudeli.co.uk

Recommended by
Isaac McHale

Opening hours...Closed Sunday
Reservation policy...No
Credit cards..Accepted
Price range...Budget
Style...Casual
Cuisine...Vietnamese
Recommended for..............................Regular neighbourhood

'Local Vietnamese baguette place. Head and shoulders
above all others I have ever tried, they have just the
right bread, layers of flavour and everything's done
really well.'—Isaac McHale

This Vietnamese deli in Shoreditch specializes in
Bánh mì, the filled baguettes that are the delicious
bastard child of Indochina's French colonial era.
Kêu, from the team behind the nearby Vietnamese
stalwarts Viet Grill and Cây Tre, have their baguettes
baked for them by the Sally Clarke bakery. They're
softer than a traditional French stick, as they should
be, despite not being made with rice flower as they
are back in Vietnam. Fillings include lemongrass-
infused mackerel with mooli and coriander; spiced
pork belly, ham terrine and chicken liver pâté; and
pork meatballs in a spicy gravy.

LEILA'S CAFÉ

17 Calvert Avenue
Shoreditch
London E2 7JP
+44 2077299789

Recommended by
Tom Adams, Neil
Borthwick, Tom Harris,
Junya Yamasaki

Opening hours	Closed Monday and Tuesday
Reservation policy	No
Credit cards	Accepted
Price range	Budget
Style	Casual
Cuisine	Café-Bistro-Deli
Recommended for	Breakfast

'Polish breakfast for me, ham and eggs for my wife, toast and jam for the kids. It doesn't get any better than this. And before we go, we'll visit Leila's shop next door which is full of all the most delicious things.'
—Tom Harris

An annexe of Lelia's Shop, which sits next door, styled like an old-fashioned grocers by virtue of the fact that that's exactly what it was until the mid-1960s, its shelves today stocked like that of a lovably eclectic delicatessen. The café has a truly open kitchen, with nothing between those cooking and the communal tables. Depending on your tolerance level, the eccentric service could at times be described as borderline surly. But that doesn't deter its loyal and fashionable following, who come for the atmosphere, the simple home-cooked dishes and the excellent coffee.

ROCHELLE CANTEEN

Rochelle School
Arnold Circus
Shoreditch
London E2 7ES
+44 2077295677
www.arnoldandhenderson.com

Recommended by
Neil Borthwick, Gabrielle
Hamilton, Miles Kirby

Opening hours	Closed Saturday and Sunday
Credit cards	Accepted
Price range	Budget
Style	Casual
Cuisine	British
Recommended for	Regular neighbourhood

'I was actually moved to eat with my fingers, suck the bones clean, and then lift the plate to my lips and drain every last drop of broth. It was unapologetically straightforward cooking.'—Gabrielle Hamilton

Occupying the converted bike sheds of a Victorian school, what began as a canteen for the local arty souls has become a Shoreditch institution. Open weekdays only, it's run by Melanie Arnold and Margot Henderson (other half of Fergus of St. John fame) and doubles up as the headquarters for their in-demand catering company. Come summertime, they set up tables outside, overlooking the school's grassy playground. The menu changes daily and is very much of the school of St. John – short, British, seasonal, tersely descriptive and delicious.

TAS FIRIN

160 Bethnal Green Road
Shoreditch
London E2 6DG
+44 2077296446

Recommended by
Tom Adams

Opening hours	Open 7 days
Reservation policy	No
Credit cards	Not accepted
Price range	Budget
Style	Casual
Cuisine	Turkish
Recommended for	Late night

'Brilliant *ocakbasi*. Great *lahmacun* (meat-topped flatbread) and *pide* (Turkish pizza) – amazing booze sponges.'—Tom Adams

TRAMSHED

Recommended by
Angela Hartnett

32 Rivington Street
Shoreditch
London EC2A 3LX
+44 2077490478
www.chickenandsteak.co.uk

Opening hours	Open 7 days
Credit cards	Accepted
Price range	Affordable
Style	Casual
Cuisine	Steakhouse
Recommended for	Regular neighbourhood

THE ANCHOR & HOPE

Recommended by
Jeremy Lee, Tom Pemberton,
Steve Williams

36 The Cut
Southwark
London SE1 8LP
+44 2079289898
www.charleswells.co.uk

Opening hours	Closed Sunday
Reservation policy	No
Credit cards	Accepted but not AMEX
Price range	Affordable
Style	Casual
Cuisine	Gastropub
Recommended for	Bargain

'Jonathan Jones writes a beautiful menu at most reasonable prices. It's brilliant, I love it and I am always happy there.'—Jeremy Lee

With its robust, well-priced cooking and decent ales, this decade-plus institution near the Old and Young Vic theatres embodies the gastropub's original (and oft-abused) virtues. Accordingly, it's more pubby than pretentious, with a plain, curtained-off dining room whose no-bookings policy usually means a longish wait in the bar for dinner. But, as you'd expect from a venture created by St. John graduates – by way of The Eagle – the cooking makes excellent use of head-to-tail ingredients in appealing dishes such as chopped rabbit and deep-fried pig's head, and non-carnivores are also well served by the daily-changing menu. Good – suitably traditional – desserts too.

MY OLD PLACE

Recommended by
Steve Williams

88–90 Middlesex Street
Spitalfields
London E1 7EZ
+44 2072472200
www.oldplace.co.uk

Opening hours	Open 7 days
Credit cards	Not accepted
Price range	Budget
Style	Casual
Cuisine	Szechuan
Recommended for	Bargain

'Fantastic Szechuan food near Liverpool Street.'
—Steve Williams

ST. JOHN BREAD & WINE

Recommended by
Tom Adams, Neil Borthwick,
Samantha & Samuel Clark,
Paul Foster, Angela Hartnett,
James Knappett, James Lowe,
Brad McDonald, Nuno Mendes,
Carlo Mirarchi, Shuko Oda,
Tom Pemberton, Andy Ricker,
Tim Siadatan, Peter Weeden,
Junya Yamasaki

94–96 Commercial Street
Spitalfields
London E1 6LZ
+44 2072510848
www.stjohngroup.uk.com

Opening hours	Open 7 days
Credit cards	Accepted
Price range	Affordable
Style	Casual
Cuisine	British
Recommended for	Local favourite

'A purely London institution. One afternoon, many years ago, I walked in and sat by myself and watched the kitchen at work. I had a dish of braised and smoked pork belly with carrots and a little bit of the braising liquid, accompanied with mustard. It was one of the most satisfying meals I have had in London.'
—Nuno Mendes

St. John's second outpost lies across from Spitalfields Market and runs a staggered, just shy of all-day, menu from breakfast – via elevenses, lunch and early afternoon nibbles – through to supper. Built around its bakery and wine shop, the cooking naturally reflects the British seasonal nose-to-tail approach that is St. John's trademark but tailors it more to tapas-style sharing. The open kitchen and bakery overlook a no-nonsense dining room, brightly lit with whitewashed walls, tightly packed with simple wooden tables and chairs. If there's one complaint, it's that the latter don't favour bony behinds.

UPSTAIRS AT THE TEN BELLS

Recommended by
Robin Gill

84 Commercial Street
Spitalfields
London E1 6LY
+44 7530492986
www.tenbells.com

Opening hours	Closed Monday
Credit cards	Accepted but not AMEX
Price range	Affordable
Style	Casual
Cuisine	Modern British
Recommended for	Local favourite

'I love that the setting is a 300-year-old public house bathed in history, but the food is as the city: modern, with mixed cultural influences and full of inspiring combinations. Most of all, I love that you feel like you are at a friend's house and totally relaxed.'—Robin Gill

HERMAN ZE GERMAN

Recommended by
Tim Siadatan

19 Villiers Street
Strand
London WC2N 6NE
www.herman-ze-german.co.uk

Opening hours	Open 7 days
Reservation policy	No
Credit cards	Accepted
Price range	Budget
Style	Casual
Cuisine	German
Recommended for	Wish I'd opened

'Great bratwurst, sauerkraut and chips. Makes me smile every time I think about it – I think it will go far.'
—Tim Siadatan

THE INDIA CLUB

Recommended by
José Pizarro

Hotel Strand Continental
143 Strand
Strand
London WC2R 1JA
+44 2078364880
www.strand-continental.co.uk

Opening hours	Open 7 days
Credit cards	Accepted
Price range	Budget
Style	Casual
Cuisine	Indian
Recommended for	Bargain

'I like the food. The staff are great. Makes me feel like I'm in India in another era. And it's BYO!'—José Pizarro

Established by India's first High Commissioner to the UK in 1946 as a meeting place for civil servants, The India Club, found up a flight of stairs off The Strand, appears to have changed little since. Portraits of Gandhi line the walls of the almost old-school classroom-like colonial canteen. A loyal clientele that ranges from students to barristers comes here for bargain dishes, from the £5 kebabs to a whole chicken for £10. Bring your own drinks (no corkage), or sip masala tea (£1.60 per cup). South Indian dishes include masala dosa, dahi vada, bhuna lamb and Mughlay chicken – with optional accompaniments of pickles and chutneys (60p).

TERROIRS

Recommended by
Tom Kerridge

5 William IV Street
Strand
London WC2N 4DW
+44 2070360660
www.terroirswinebar.com

Opening hours	Closed Sunday
Credit cards	Accepted
Price range	Affordable
Style	Casual
Cuisine	French
Recommended for	Bargain

'Brilliant, rustic French cooking, simple terrines and great pork products.'—Tom Kerridge

BRAVI RAGAZZI

Recommended by
Matthew Harris

2a Sunnyhill Road
Streatham
London SW16 2UH
+44 2087694966
www.braviragazzipizzeria.co.uk

Opening hours	Open 7 days
Reservation policy	No
Credit cards	Accepted but not AMEX
Price range	Budget
Style	Casual
Cuisine	Pizza
Recommended for	Late night

'Great sourdough pizza.'—Matthew Harris

LAHORE KEBAB HOUSE

Recommended by
Atul Kochhar

2–10 Umberston Street
Whitechapel
London E1 1PY
+44 2074819737
www.lahore-kebabhouse.com

Opening hours	Open 7 days
Credit cards	Accepted
Price range	Budget
Style	Casual
Cuisine	Pakistani
Recommended for	Bargain

'Serves the best traditional Indian food in London without a doubt. The lamb chops – they're famous for a reason!'—Atul Kochar

TAYYABS

Recommended by
Ollie Dabbous, Henry Harris

83–89 Fieldgate Street
Whitechapel
London E1 1JU
+44 2072479543
www.tayyabs.co.uk

Opening hours	Open 7 days
Credit cards	Accepted
Price range	Budget
Style	Casual
Cuisine	Indian-Pakistani
Recommended for	Bargain

'Grilled lamb chops, dry meat curry and naan. Great buzz, always a queue and it's BYO.'
—Henry Harris

No one comes to Tayyabs for the ambience. Forty years after opening, E1's worst-kept secret is more cut and thrust than ever, from the location round the back of Whitechapel High Street to the hour-plus queues – and that's with a reservation – and the ferocious noise levels. However, the Punjabi food – specifically the sizzling lamb chops and groaning mixed grill plate, as well as fresh-from-the-tandoor naan – makes it all worthwhile, especially with change from £20. Don't get caught out by the BYO policy – bring an extra beer or two so you can enjoy a pre-dinner drink while you wait for a table.

INDEX BY RESTAURANT

INDEX BY TYPE

County Galway
  Kai Café & Restaurant 49
County of Inverness
  Rocpool 37
County Waterford
  The House Restaurant 50
East Sussex
  The Landgate Bistro 29
Greater Manchester
  The Parlour 29
Jersey
  The Bass & Lobster 36
  Siam Garden 36
Kent
  David Brown Delicatessen 31
  Raj Bari 31
London
  Acton
    North China 54
  Barnes
    Riva 54
    Sonny's Kitchen 54
  Battersea
    Augustine Kitchen 54
  Belgravia
    Tinello 56
  Bermondsey
    40 Maltby Street 90
    José 90
    Zucca 91
  Bloomsbury
    Ciao Bella 91
  Borough
    Hutong 92
    Magdalen 92
  Chelsea
    Le Colombier 57
    Made in Italy 57
    Medlar 57
  Chiswick
    La Trompette 59
  City of London
    Moshi Moshi 94
  Clerkenwell
    Morito 96
    Moro 96
  Ealing
    Maxim Chinese Restaurant 60
  Hackney
    Lardo 101
    Raw Duck 102
    The Windsor Castle 103
  Hoxton
    Brawn 103
  Islington
    Smokehouse 106

  Trullo 106
  Kensal Green
    Dock Kitchen 61
    Parlour Kensal 62
  Knightsbridge
    Koffmann's 63
  Marylebone
    Bistrot de Luxe 63
    Le Relais de Venise 65
    Texture 66
  Mayfair
    Gymkhana 77
    Princess Garden of Mayfair 80
  Notting Hill
    Hereford Road 67
  Parsons Green
    Tendido Cuatro 67
  Shoreditch
    Burro e Salvia 107
    Kêu Bánh Mì Deli 108
    Rochelle Canteen 109
    Tramshed 110
  Soho
    Barrafina 82
    Bocca di Lupo 82
    Ducksoup 84
    Quo Vadis 86
    Randall & Aubin 86
    Wright Brothers 87
  Wimbledon
    Sticks'n'Sushi 70
Powys
  The Felin Fach Griffin 40
Vale of Glamorgan
  The Fig Tree 40
West Midlands
  The Malt Shovel 35
Wiltshire
  Red Lion Freehouse 35

WISH I'D OPENED
Ceredigion
  The Harbourmaster 39
Cornwall
  The Seafood Restaurant 25
County Clare
  Wild Honey Inn 43
County Cork
  Fishy Fishy Café 45
Durham
  The Raby Hunt Restaurant 28
Hampshire
  The Black Rat Restaurant 30
London
  Bayswater
    Khans 55

City of London
  Barbecoa 94
Fitzrovia
  Berners Tavern 99
  Bubbledogs 99
  Dabbous 100
  Honey & Co. 100
  Kitchen Table 100
King's Cross
  Caravan 106
Knightsbridge
  Amaya 62
  Zuma 63
Mayfair
  Bentley's Oyster Bar
    & Grill 75
  Brasserie Chavot 76
  La Petite Maison 79
  Pollen Street Social 80
  Scott's 80
Notting Hill
  Electric Diner 66
Shoreditch
  The Clove Club 107
  Fifteen 108
Soho
  Polpo 85
Strand
  Herman Ze German 111
Tooting
  The Little Bar 70
Oxfordshire
  Le Manoir Aux Quat'Saisons 32
Somerset
  The Ethicurean 34

WORTH THE TRAVEL
Argyll
  The Hawthorn Restaurant 37
Bristol
  Casamia 25
Cheshire
  Sticky Walnut 25
County Clare
  Dining Room 43
County Dublin
  Chapter One 46
Cumbria
  L'Enclume 27
Dorset
  Hix Oyster & Fish House 28
Edinburgh
  The Kitchin 37
Essex
  The Company Shed 29
Gloucestershire

  Le Champignon Sauvage 29
Kent
  The Sportsman 31
London
  Chiswick
    Hedone 58
  Knightsbridge
    Dinner by Heston
      Blumenthal 62
  Mayfair
    Coya 76
    Hibiscus 78
    Nobu 79
  Peckham
    The Begging Bowl 106
  Soho
    Yauatcha 88
Monmouthshire
  The Walnut Tree 40
Nottinghamshire
  Restaurant Sat Bains 32

NOTES

NOTES

Phaidon Press Limited
Regent's Wharf
All Saints Street
London N1 9PA

Phaidon Press Inc.
65 Bleecker Street
New York, NY 10012

www.phaidon.com

First published in 2015
© 2015 Phaidon Press Limited

This special edition of Where Chefs Eat was
created exclusively for Waterstones

ISBN 978 0 7148 7102 8

A CIP catalogue record for this book
is available from the British Library.

As many restaurants are closed Sunday and/or
Monday, and some change their opening hours
in relation to the seasons or close for extended
periods at different times of the year, it is always
advisable to check opening hours before visiting.
All information is correct at the time of going to
print, but is subject to change.

Commissioning Editor: Emilia Terragni
Project Editors: Sophie Hodgkin and Elizabeth Clinton
Contributing Editor: Joe Warwick
Production Controller: Lena Hall

Designed by Kobi Benezri

The publisher would like to thank all the participating
chefs for their generosity, time and insightful
restaurant recommendations; Joe Warwick for
his commitment and enthusiasm; and Imogen
Adams, Hilary Armstrong, Douglas Blyde, Adam
Browne, Sophie Chatellier, Daniel Chehade, Colin
Christie, Sophie Dening, Lena Hall, Corinna
Hardgrave, Anne Heining, Anna Kibbey, Clodagh
Kinsella, Andy Lynes, Ana Minguez, Laura Nickoll,
Chris Pople, Nick Redgrove, Emma Robertson,
Tracey Smith, Emma Sturgess, Oliver Thring and
Maria Zizka for their contributions to the book.

Printed in Italy